Merry Christmas Father

From Al Salesburg

PACIFIC
TUGBOATS

PACIFIC
TUGBOATS

by
GORDON NEWELL

Photographs from the JOE WILLIAMSON *Marine Collection*

SUPERIOR   PUBLISHING   COMPANY   •   SEATTLE

AUTOGRAPHED EDITION

Two thousand copies of this autographed
edition have been printed
This copy is Number

_998_

Gordon Newell

4

To the men of the Pacific Coast's
fleet of working boats, and to the memory of a
courageous man who told their story well, Stewart
C. Osborn . . . "Scuttlebutt Pete" . . . this book is
dedicated.

FOREWORD

THIS book does not cover the subject of tugboating on the West Coast. It would take a library full of books this size to do that. It does try to present a representative sampling of the subject, and we have tried to make it an honest sampling. As accurately as we could, we have assembled the highlights of a century of towboating . . . some drama, some comedy, some tragedy.

Whether they're bulling their way through mile-a-minute storms to find some stricken ship a thousand miles at sea or slogging down the fairway on a summer afternoon with seagulls hitching sleepy rides on the boom of logs astern, the tugboats are a colorful and essential part of the Pacific Coast seascape today, just as they were a century ago.

The hiss of steam and the creak of walking-beams have given way to the efficient rumble of the diesel, but the tugboats' story is still a tale of men in little ships who aren't afraid to take on a mighty big ocean. Their daily routine tasks provide countless tales of hard-hitting sea adventure to rival the exploits of the great ships, sail and steam alike.

The pictures came mostly from the thousands of negatives in the files of Joe Williamson's Marine Photo Shop collection. Many were taken by Joe himself, others by working tugboat men. Not all of them are the kind of perfect photographs that win awards in salon shows ashore, but salon photographers don't have to focus a spray-streaked lens on the reeling deck of a hundred-footer in the teeth of a North Pacific storm. A lot of pretty pictures were discarded in favor of somewhat blurry ones that did a better job of telling the tugboat story.

The stories came mostly from those best qualified to tell them . . . the men who run the tugboats. Here's a partial list of the fine crew who helped bring *Pacific Tugboats* safe to port:

Capt. Otto Johnson, Washington Tug and Barge, Capt. Louis Van Bogaert, Washington State Ferries, D. B. Elworthy, Island Tug & Barge, Jay J. Kalee, U.S. Army Engineers, Oswald H. (Sparkie) New, Coastal Towing Company, C. A. MacNeill, Jr., Western Transportation Company, Capts. John H. and Charles W. Cates, C. H. Cates and Sons, James A. Gibbs, Jr., maritime writer, and Capt. E. I. Jocz.

C. Arthur and Henry Foss, Foss Launch and Tug Company, Capt. Art Torgesen, Foss Launch and Tug Company, H. W. McCurdy, Puget Sound Bridge and Dredging Company, J. A. Lundie, Powell River Company (Kingcome Navigation Company), Perry Moore, Foss Launch and Tug Company, John Olson, Olson Tug Boat Company, Capt. Volney Young, Capital City Tugboat Company, Dr. George A. Stansfield, formerly of the *Zephyr*, and Capt. Fred G. Lewis, formerly of the *Sarah Dixon*.

One thing is certain; there is material for more tugboat books. We hope some day to write them. We would like very much to hear from readers who have pictures or stories they think should be included in future tales of the Pacific tugboats.

One of the things we like best about tugboating is its friendliness and informality. Nobody wears gold braid and the coffee's always hot in the galley. So, to those who have suggestions for future tugboat books . . . *welcome aboard!*

HIS MAJESTY THE TUG BOAT

(Dedicated to a Winner and a Sport)
The Liner — she's a lady; that's the reason why, no doubt,
She always needs assistance gettin' in an' gettin' out;
She can't come up the river and she dassn't dock alone
So she whistles for a tugboat in a most implorin' tone,
An' the tugboat takes the hawser an' his wake begins to boil
With his engine chuggin' lively and consumin' Diesel oil.
Then he swings her and he pulls her — like a cowboy drivin' stock,
An' he hasn't got no manners — but he gets her to the dock.

When there's any job to tackle he will take it anyhow
Whether towin' racin' liners or a garbage scow.
You will see him ploddin' heavy with a raft of rollin' logs,
Or a-chuggin' down the harbor with a barge of squealin' hogs,
With a string of empty lighters or a ship from 'round the Horn,
With a fleet of pleasure barges or a freighter full of corn,
He yanks them through the river an' his husky whistle blows
As he tells the wayward steamer to be lookin' where she goes.

The Tug — he bucks the river when it's full of grindin' ice,
An' when there's trade to handle, why, you needn't call him twice,
For he's there a ridin' combers maybe fifty miles at sea
An' he doesn't stop for danger when he's lookin' for a fee;
He's a little giant helper, he's the live wire of the port,
He's a nervy, nifty snorter an' a winner an' a sport,
He's the snubby-nosed exploiter of the chances of the game
An' he's never much on beauty, but he gets there just the same.

(Author unknown)

THE PIONEERS

The first tugboat to come to the Pacific Coast wasn't built for that purpose, although she did a bit of towing along with other more colorful tasks during her early years. She ended her days more than half a century after her arrival, however, as a full-time and peculiarly unlovely towboat.

The *Beaver,* built at London for the Hudson's Bay Company, sailed up to the Columbia River Bar in the early spring of 1836. She sailed in the literal sense—under canvas—because she couldn't carry enough fuel to get her from London to the Lizard, much less across the ocean under steam. She made the voyage, by way of the "Sandwich Islands", in 163 days. It was no world's record passage, but she did beat the company's regular Oregon to England packet, the bark *Columbia,* and she made history in the bargain.

After her arrival at Fort Vancouver, engineers assembled her wood and iron side-wheels well forward on her stubby 101-foot hull. Then they fired up the boilers of her two side-lever engines to their full working pressure of two and a half pounds to the square inch.

The *Beaver* wasn't far removed from the era of Robert Fulton's *Clermont* . . . her engines had been built by the same firm that built the *Clermont's* as a matter of fact . . . and she was

"THE LINER, SHE'S A LADY, and that is why, no doubt she always needs assistance in getting in and out." . . . Government and commercial tugs ease the big transport **Fuller** through the Lake Washington Ship Canal at Seattle.

slow and greedy. Although her engines weighed many tons they developed only 75 horsepower and devoured whole forests of wood in the process. A chopping crew of ten men had to travel with her where ever she went and she spent as much time "fueling up" as she did steaming.

But the *Beaver* was the first steamboat to navigate the waters of America's West Coast. As such, she earned a solid place in history, but not in the heart of Dr. John McLoughlin, Scots factor of the Hudson's Bay post at Vancouver. Her expensive habits gave him the horrors; furthermore, McLoughlin had a theory that most, if not all, sailors were given to drinking rum and breaking windows. All in all, he considered the *Beaver* and her crew a doubtful blessing. Before long he sent her, with his compliments, to his colleague at Fort Nisqually on Puget Sound, Dr. William Tolmie.

Tolmie put her to work at a little of everything, from swapping for furs with Northwest Indians to towing company windjammers to Puget Sound ports. Some of her Indian customers had piratical tendencies, so the *Beaver* carried a battery of little brass cannon in those days; her crew of wood-choppers were trained to do emergency duty as man-o'-warsmen.

In later years the historic little *Beaver* served as a Canadian government survey boat, as a passenger and freight packet and, for many years, as a tug. Stripped of her auxiliary sails as well as her jaunty brass cannon and straining away at heavy log booms, she outlived her

THE HISTORIC BEAVER came to the Pacific Coast in 1836. When she ran aground at Vancouver more than fifty years later she might have lived to sail again if souvenir-hunters hadn't stripped her of most of her fittings.

adventurous era, but she never outlived her usefulness. She was still hard at work when, in 1888, she hit the rocks at the entrance to Vancouver, B. C. harbor.

The stout oaken hull wasn't badly damaged, but the old *Beaver* was so famous by that time that everyone wanted a souvenir from the "first steamer". She was almost torn apart by people who admired her so much that they helped to end her life. Pieces of the unfortunate *Beaver* are still to be found scattered all over the Pacific Coast.

The bare hull lay forlornly on the rocks for four years until the big side-wheeler *Yosemite* came ramping into port on the crest of a high June tide in 1892. The *Yosemite's* swell swept over the tired old *Beaver* and the little pioneer was gone. She was, among a lot of other things, the first tugboat on the west coast of America.

The *Beaver* lived a respectable and hard-working life and it was not until 17 years after

her arrival that another Hudson's Bay steamer came along to uphold Dr. McLoughlin's convictions about sailors. The *Otter* came from England to join the *Beaver* in 1853. It was still a long voyage and so elated was the *Otter's* master at having made his landfall off Cape Flattery that he broke out the grog prematurely.

He had planned a modest celebration, but his impromptu party gained so much headway that the *Otter* lost hers entirely. The crew got higher and higher as the boiler pressure dropped lower and lower. The *Otter* just drifted sideways into the Strait of Juan de Fuca, like a trustworthy horse that can find its own way home but goes about it in its own way.

Fortunately the weather was pleasant, the winds and current favorable, so she slogged along peacefully until the crew sobered up sufficiently to take over again.

Steam wasn't quite such a novelty on the

EARLY SEA GOING TUGS like the **Kamishak** were often built without pilot houses. This custom was abandoned when the **Columbia's** steering wheel and skipper were both washed overboard in a storm off the Columbia River bar.

Pacific Coast by the 1850's and, sensational as it was, the *Otter's* arrival didn't cause nearly the sensation the *Beaver's* had . . . except among the Indians. They could understand how the

Beaver's husky paddle-wheels chunked against the water to send her trundling along, but the *Otter* was a screw steamer. Her propeller was out of sight under several feet of water and it took the Indians a long time to figure out what made her *mamook*.

In the meantime, a real tugboat had put in an appearance on San Francisco Bay. The *Goliah,* a 136-foot sidewheeler, was built at New York in 1849. She was the second tug ever built in the United States and the largest in the world at that time. She was owned by Commodore Vanderbilt for a time, but not proving quite satisfactory for his purposes, was sold.

The new owners ran into debt and the sturdy *Goliah* was tied to a dock with a libel notice tacked to her pilot house. A sheriff's deputy was placed aboard to see that she did no work with which to pay her debts. In the normal course of events the *Goliah* would have been sold at auction to satisfy her creditors, but

there was a gold rush on in California and she had a hardy crew.

When the ship's jailer went ashore for a quick beer the *Goliah's* crew got up a quick head of steam and started for San Francisco. That meant a circumnavigation of two continents by way of Cape Horn in a paddle-wheel harbor tug. It also meant that the *Goliah's* crew were pirates, but one problem seemed to bother them as little as the other.

No one seems to know quite how they made it, but make it they did, and the *Goliah's* jinx seemed to have been washed overboard somewhere along the Cape Horn Road, for she ran successfully as a coastwise passenger steamer from San Francisco to Humboldt and the Pacific Northwest, as a Sacramento River passenger boat and as a bay tug. She was abandoned on the Mission mudflats for a while in the 1860's, but she went back to bay towing in 1864, sticking to it until 1871, when she went to Puget Sound to begin a new life as the first unit in a great fleet of logging tugs to be operated by the Pope and Talbot sawmill empire. She was also the first of an almost continuous line of tugboats named *Goliah,* a Puget Sound tradition which has continued almost to the present time.

TUGBOAT TURNED PIRATE. The first **Goliah** ran away from the New York sheriff to round Cape Horn under her own power. The second real tugboat built in America, she was active at San Francisco and on Puget Sound from 1850 to 1899.

The *Goliah* was skippered by one of the West's most famous tugboat men, Capt. S. D. Libby, who was a hard man to beat at his own game—tugboating. On one occasion he and Capt. Chris Williams of the old tug *Tacoma* found themselves bidding against each other for the job of towing a British bark in from

Cape Flattery. Capt. Williams figured he had "Old Man Libby" whipped when he finally offered to tow the windship in free gratis and for nothing.

But Cap Libby's dander was up. "I'll tow you in for nothing . . . and buy you a new hat in the bargain!" he roared at the delighted shipmaster. The *Goliah* got the tow and the British skipper got his new hat.

Capt. Libby recouped his losses shortly thereafter, however. The *Goliah* waddled out to meet a big Scandinavian bark which had come ramping sweetly up to Juan de Fuca entrance on the wings of a perfect Southwesterly. The tight-fisted shipmaster figured he could count on the wind, which was free. He scornfully turned down Libby's offer to take him in for $150.

When the *Goliah* turned back toward port that evening, still without a tow, Capt. Libby spotted the Scandinavian bark hanging on by both anchors and a prayer within spitting distance of Vancouver Island's deadly reefs. The tight-fisted master had been learning a great

deal about the vagaries of wind and currents in the vicinity of Cape Flattery, but in the course of his education his ship had ended up on a dead lee shore with no room left for maneuvering. The captain caused blue lights to be shown and prayed that his anchors would hold for a while.

They were still holding when the *Goliah* came rolling up alongside and Capt. Libby poked his leathery face out an open pilot house window to renew negotiations.

"I've decided to take that offer of yours to tow me in for $150", the shipmaster shouted, trying not to look at the spouting rocks so close astern.

"The price is $500!" Capt. Libby roared back.

"But that's robbery!" screamed the outraged Scandinavian. "I'm furder in than I was when you offered to do the job for $150!"

"In more ways than one", Libby agreed. "The wind's picking up, too, so I'll just wait a while. When your anchors start to drag, the price goes up to a thousand".

The bark's master cast his cap upon the deck and danced on it, but when he was through dancing he took the *Goliah's* hawser. And Cap Libby took his $500.

A full-time tugboat had come to Puget Sound to tow logs a good many years before the *Goliah* first headed north from San Francisco. This pioneer craft, the 90-foot sidewheeler *Resolute*, was a native of Philadelphia which, like the *Goliah*, had joined the California gold rush. She arrived at San Francisco in 1850 and on Puget Sound in 1858. On the Sound she settled down to a toilsome career of log towing for Meiggs' Port Madison Mill Company.

She was still at it ten years later, yanking bravely at a great boom of logs on the upper Sound. Her heart was still stout but the stress and strain of the years had weakened her boiler. It cut loose with a blast that could be heard in Olympia, seven miles away. Only the skipper, Johnny Guindon, and his mate survived the explosion and Johnny was badly mauled and scalded.

As the first professional tugboat pilot in the Pacific Northwest, Guindon's place in the hearts of all workboat men should be secure. He made it doubly so when he aroused himself from his bed of pain and bottle of pain-killer at Olympia's Pacific House to dispatch his classic telegram to the boss at Port Madison:

"*Resolute blown up. Boom gone to hell. And I'm at the Pacific Hotel.*"

The *Resolute* was replaced by a ship with a personality and a past as colorful as the *Beaver's*. Her name was *Politkofsky*, but no one on Puget Sound could pronounce it, let alone spell it, so she became just plain *Polly*.

Polly had started life in Alaska as a gunboat of the Imperial Russian Navy; had been thrown in with the rest of the country when Alaska was purchased by the United States. Among other peculiarities, she was equipped with a fine battery of iron cannon which would have made her more than a match for the *Beaver*. She also had a pure copper boiler, which was

FAMOUS OLDTIMER on both Puget Sound and San Francisco Bay was the sidewheel tugboat **Favorite**. Built at Utsalady, Washington, in 1869, the **Favorite** spent most of her long life towing logs for the Puget Mill Company. She lasted until World War I days and was always kept as neat and trim as a yacht.

sold in San Francisco for more than her owners paid the government for the entire ship. Even in 1868 there was a nice profit to be made in government surplus deals.

Progress manifested itself on the Columbia River Bar as early as 1865, when Capt. Paul Corno brought the 100-foot steam tug *Rabonni* from San Francisco to set up shop as bar tug and pilot boat. Things looked bad for Capt. Flavel, who had maintained a monopoly in bar piloting with old-fashioned pilot schooners.

It soon developed, however, that deepwater windship skippers had a distrust of steamboats. They rejected the *Rabonni's* services. Business was so bad that Corno had to take his steam tug back to San Francisco and it was another four years before Flavel built a steamer to replace his wind-powered pilot boats. His tug *Astoria*, built in 1869, still resembled a schooner as much as a steamboat. She had a deckhouse and a funnel, but she also had two tall masts rigged for sail. She had no pilot house, her steering wheel being mounted aft on the open deck in traditional sailing ship style.

The later bar tugs *C. J. Brenham* and *Columbia* were built on the same lines, but tradition got a rude jolt one unpleasant night when a huge sea came aboard the *Columbia*, removing both wheel and skipper from the after deck. Neither was ever seen again and the *Columbia* was equipped with a strong pilot house forward, anchored clear down to the keel with iron rods.

The pattern for both tugs and tugboating was becoming established.

SAILING DROUGHERS of the coastal lumber fleet kept tugs like Capt. Flavel's **Columbia** busy along the West Coast river and harbor bars. (Note helmsman at the big wheel aft on tug's deck without protection from wind or weather.)

THE OREGON BAR TUG TRIUMPH proves that towboating is no job for ribbon clerks as she bulldozes a three-masted lumber drougher across the Coos Bay bar. Styles in ships have changed in the 70 years since this picture was taken . . . but the sea hasn't.

THE MIGHTY SALVAGE KING deep-sea salvage tug of the Straits Towing Company, at work in Vancouver harbor. The **Salvage King** burned and sank in Victoria harbor in October, 1953, but has since been raised.

TUG ACTIVE, owned by Coastal Towing Co., Ltd., aground on Cortes Island, off Campbell River, V.I., B.C., June 26, 1956; she was refloated and towed back to Victoria by **Island Champion,** June 29, 1956.—(Photo courtesy Island Tug and Barge, Ltd.)

A UNIT OF THE RUSSIAN NAVY in pre-Civil War days, the old **Politkofsky** was thrown in with the rest of Alaska when the Czar sold that northern territory to the United States. For many years a towboat on Puget Sound, the ancient **Polly** ended her days about 1906 as a barge on the Yukon River.

PUGET SOUND

Tugboating started on Puget Sound as a means of getting trees to the mills. The "timber barons" of the nineteenth century built their sawmills on tidewater, ringed with miles of virgin forests, but the headsaws screamed day and night and the appetite of the mills was never satisfied. Deeper they ate into the primeval forests and ever deeper. Logs had to be brought to the mills from more distant forests still uncut and the old steam tugs towed the rafts to the mills.

Sailing ships came to Puget Sound from all ports of the world; around the Horn from Europe and East Coast ports, across the Pacific from the Orient and the Antipodes, up the coast from the booming towns of California.

It was important to get the logs to the mills, but it was important to get the cargo ships to the mill docks too. A ship could make her landfall at Cape Flattery and then spend weeks beating up and down the coast trying to get inside. It would have been fine if each big mill company could afford to keep a tug cruising the cape all the time, but none of them could. Furthermore, there were unprofitable rivalries like the one between Captain Libby of Puget Mill's *Goliah* and Captain Williams of Tacoma Mill's *Tacoma*.

Under the circumstances, cooperation seemed not only desirable but essential. By early 1891 four of the largest mills had formed a tugboat "pool", each contributing one boat from its fleet. The Port Blakely Mill the *Wanderer*, the Tacoma Mill the *Tacoma*, the Washington Mill

Company the *Richard Holyoke*, and the Puget Mill Company the giant *Tyee*, built at Port Ludlow in 1884 as the most powerful tug in the United States.

Those four boats formed the first large organized towing company on the Sound . . . the historic Puget Sound Tug Boat Company. All of them were far removed from the original wood-burning sidewheelers. They burned coal instead of wood and powerful reciprocating engines turned their big propellers. Most of them worked their way far into the twentieth century.

At the turn of the century, when the company moved its headquarters from Port Townsend to Seattle, it boasted a fleet of nine big tugs: the *Wanderer*, Capt. Buck Bailey, the *Tyee*, Capt. William Gove, the *Tacoma*, Capt. J. S. Bollong, the *Richard Holyoke*, Capt. F. W. Clinger, the *Pioneer*, Capt. Tom Neilson, the *Sea Lion*, Capt. C. C. Manter, the *Magic*, Capt. H. H. Morrison, and the *Lorne*, Capt. C. H. Locke. Capt. Libby of *Goliah* fame was company manager and he prided himself on paying top scale for tugboat crews . . . $200 a month to masters, 150 to chief engineers, 90 to assistant engineers, 75 to mates,

OFF CAPE FLATTERY, a Puget Sound tug prepares to drop her line from the American bark **Burgess.** Puget Sound Tug Boat Company boats kept 150 fathoms of manila line and 30 fathoms of wire cable between their towing bitts and the ship astern as a minimum rule. A long hawser obviates sudden jerks and lessens the strain on both ship and tug.

WITH A BONE IN HER TEETH and coal smoke pouring from her tall stack, the big **Tyee** plows down the Strait of Juan de Fuca toward the open sea. The 140-foot **Tyee** was built for Pope and Talbot at Port Ludlow in 1884, designed to the specifications of the mill company's Northwest manager, Cyrus Walker, and built by Hiram Doncaster a n d William McCurdy, who had learned the art of shipbuilding in the clipper shipyards of Donald McKay.

CLASSIC DEEP - SEA STEAM TUGS of Puget Sound Tug Boat Company, the **Wallowa** and **Prosper,** moored at Seattle's old Pier 2.

BIG BRITISH COLUMBIA STEAM TUG CZAR, stationed across the Strait of Juan de Fuca from the Port Townsend based Puget Sound Tug Boat Company fleet, was a frequent rival of Capt. Libby's tugs during the days of sail. Like the American tugs, the **Czar** braved mountainous North Pacific seas in epic rescue and salvage operations off Cape Flattery and Vancouver Island.

PUGET SOUND TUG Boat Company's **Richard Holyoke,** veteran of many tussles with huge Cape Horn square-riggers, found the going easy when she helped the little schooner **Vega** out to sea. The **Richard Holyoke,** built at Seabeck in 1877, made many voyages to Alaska, towing ore barges and, in later years, serving as a tender to the fishing fleet. During the Alaska Gold Rush the **Holyoke** towed two famous Puget Sound craft, the **W. K. Merwin** and the **Politkofsky,** to the mouth of the Yukon River.

TATOOSH ON HER MAIDEN VOYAGE.

50 to cooks and firemen, 40 to deckhands.

He prided himself on first class service, too. Four of the tugs cruised the cape continually, one 15 miles at sea, a second 10 miles off the cape, another five miles off and the fourth lying "under the cape". Inbound ships seldom had to wait for a tug.

Outward bound the Puget Sound tugs took their ships well clear of dangerous Cape Flattery, usually from ten to twenty miles out to

STEAM SCHOONER WASHINGTON

sea. San Francisco tugs of that era "hooked" a ship in the harbor and towed her past the ninth buoy, a distance of only eight miles.

Captain Libby was fond of observing that his tugs gave towed vessels a greater "offing" than the entire tow of most San Francisco boats.

THE MIGHTY TATOOSH

The Puget Sound Tug Boat Company went a step beyond the wood-hulled *Tyee* when, in 1899, Captain Libby placed an order with the Moran Shipyard at Seattle for a new steel boat to be named *Tatoosh*.

The *Tatoosh*, completed in eight months and launched on February 22, 1900, cost the unheard of sum of $80,000. She was planned as the finest tug on the West Coast and her designers did their work well. She was destined for great things.

Captain Buck Bailey rode his new craft down the ways at her launching, along with Chief Engineer Primrose, Mate Williams and the rest of the new tug's crew, twelve men in all. The launching went off without a hitch amid flags in profusion and the martial strains of "Dad" Wagner's First Regiment Band.

Thus gaily launched, the 128-foot tug was moved to the outfitting dock to receive her two scotch boilers, big triple-expansion engine, and "all modern improvements and conveniences, including electric lights, steam heat, searchlights, and an independent donkey boiler of sufficient capacity to furnish steam for all her auxiliary machinery". In mid-July the *Tatoosh,* well supplied with flags, food and liquid refreshments, made her trial run to Port Townsend at an easy 14 knot speed (faster than any modern diesel tug has gone in the post-war International Tugboat Races at Seattle). Speeches were made by builder Robert Moran and ex-governor John McGraw and afterward "an elegant lunch was served in the cabin and a testimonial presented to Captain Libby by those aboard".

After that the *Tatoosh* began the career of hard work which is the destiny of any self-respecting tugboat. By 1907 she was on station at the mouth of the Columbia River as a bar tug. In the course of her duties there she saved dozens of ships from probable or certain disaster. Her most spectacular feat was the brink-of-disaster rescue of the steam schooner *Washington* from the graveyard of Peacock Spit.

FORTY-EIGHT DOOMED!

SCHOONER WASHINGTON DRIVEN ASHORE!
GALE CATCHES HELPLESS VESSEL EMERGING FROM COLUMBIA RIVER

Schooner Smashed Down on Reef by Heavy Seas, Then Slowly but Surely Carried on to Destruction---Lifesavers and Tugs Unable to Reach Those Aboard Battered Hulk

NEWSPAPER ACCOUNTS listed the steam schooner **Washington** as "doomed," but the tug **Tatoosh,** with Capt. Buck Bailey at the helm, went into the surf to snatch the little ship to safety in a nick-of-time rescue which was recorded in the old news photograph (below), taken from North Head by a Seattle **Times** photographer.

BAHADA WAS LAUNCHED IN 1903 along with her sister tug **Wyadda.** After a 23-year career in Washington and California waters she was lost with all her crew in a mysterious disaster on Puget Sound.

The *Washington*, a typical wooden lumber carrier, was built at Seattle in 1906. She was registered at 539 gross tons. Although built primarily to haul lumber, her after deckhouse had accommodations of a sort for 36 passengers.

The *Washington's* holds and decks were crammed with half a million feet of spruce lumber when she left her Portland, Oregon dock on November 11, 1911, bound for San Francisco. She carried 25 passengers and a crew of 24. This was the absolute maximum she was allowed as she had no wireless and it was compulsory for vessels carrying 50 or more persons to have this safeguard.

The *Washington's* skipper, Capt. George Winkel, held her up at Astoria for a while because the bar was breaking. By noon the next day

things looked quieter and the little steamer headed seaward between the long stone jetties. "We passed the south channel buoy without even wetting the foc'sle head", Capt. Winkel recalled afterward.

Then a single vast wave, roaring in from the sea overwhelmed the little ship without warning. When it passed the *Washington* was a helplessly drifting hulk, her deck load torn loose, her hull strained and leaking and her engines dead. The scrambled timbers of the deck load forced her far over to starboard. Broken cable lashings had apparently fouled her propeller to keep her engine from turning over. The big comber had been the forerunner of a fast-rising gale and the *Washington* began wallowing toward the line of surf marking deadly Peacock

THE PIONEER, shown here alongside the bark **Alfield,** was built at Philadelphia in 1878. A few years later she came around the Horn for a try at breaking the towing monopoly on the Columbia River. Most of her career was spent on Puget Sound where she was the last of the old Puget Sound Tug Boat Company fleet in active service.

Spit at the foot of Cape Disappointment.

She had no wireless. By the time her plight was discovered the storm winds were blowing seventy miles an hour and the bar was a welter of churned sand and surf. The bar tugs *Oneonta, Wallula, Goliah* and *Tatoosh* were inside and couldn't get out. The Coast Guardsmen from the Canby Station were just as helpless. That night city newspapers announced that the *Washington* was doomed and those aboard her given up for dead.

At dawn the next morning Bailey saw the *Washington* still above water, although apparently right in the line of breakers. A veteran bar pilot warned him, "Don't try it, Captain. That's the most treacherous spot on the coast in there. All you'll do is pile up alongside the

schooner."

Buck Bailey listened politely; then reached for the bell-pulls. The *Tatoosh* headed for the breaking bar. The *Oneonta* trailed her part way, then turned back. The *Tatoosh*, alone, disappeared in the wet murk at the river mouth.

Afterward watchers on Cape Disappointment saw the *Tatoosh* come in out of the sea mist, warily stalking the doomed *Washington*. There was little room for errors and Bailey took no unnecessary chances. It was three o'clock in the afternoon before he was close enough to risk firing a line. The first three lines were whipped away by the storm. Time was running out. The life of the *Washington* and those aboard her literally hung by a thread.

A fourth puff of smoke from the *Tatoosh's* Lyle-gun and in minutes a thin line rose dripping from the sea to grow taut between the steam schooner and the tug. They crossed the bar on the crest of the flood tide; the battered, waterlogged hulk of the *Washington* was in quiet waters, every soul aboard safe and thankful.

THE FOSS STORY

The old Puget Sound Tug Boat Company started big, as nineteenth century towing companies went, and it grew even bigger, but it had a limited purpose in life. Its purpose was the towing of ocean sailing vessels to mill docks on sheltered inland waters. When the world's sailing fleet declined and vanished from the seas the legendary Puget Sound Tug Boat Company declined and eventually vanished also. The firm was mostly a paper corporation after 1919 and in 1926 it sold its only remaining tug, the *Pioneer,* to the Chas. R. McCormick Lumber Company.

The company which was eventually to take its place as the biggest towing firm in the Pacific Northwest—and one of the biggest in the United States—had started operations two years before the Puget Sound Tug Boat Company was formed. It's called the Foss Launch and Tug Company now, but it had no special name back in 1889, nor did it own a single tugboat. Like the big company of those days, its business was with the sailing ships of the grain and lumber fleets, but as times changed Foss operations changed with them.

Andrew Foss started life in America as a carpenter in Minnesota, but after eight years in the Midwest he joined the growing tide of migration toward the Pacific. He stopped off in the Rocky Mountains for a while to work with a Northern Pacific Railway construction crew. Then he moved on toward tidewater. His final stop was at Tacoma.

Like most of those who migrated westward, Andrew Foss was looking for land of his own.

He wanted to be a farmer, but his destiny seemed to be linked with the sea. His first job in Tacoma was on a boat of the Tacoma Tug and Barge Company. He sent for his wife, Thea, and the children, but when their fares were paid there wasn't enough money left to rent much of a house. Andrew found a deserted fisherman's shack on the waterfront. It could be had for a few dollars and it became the family's first home on Puget Sound.

Andrew found a better job in a Tacoma shipyard. His brothers, Ivar and Peter, had come west too, and they were working in a sawmill. Ivar and Peter were good with machinery and Andrew was a fine carpenter, so they decided that instead of waiting for their ship to come in they would build it for themselves . . . in their spare time.

They bought the rusty engines and boiler from a little steamboat called the *St. Patrick,* stranded on a sandbar in the bay. These they installed in a new hull built by Andrew Foss. Their boat, the *Blue Star,* was the first ship of the Foss fleet, but the brothers had built her to sell, not to operate. The *Blue Star* led a long and useful life on Puget Sound, but not under Foss ownership.

It was Thea, Andrew's wife, who really founded the fleet. While Andrew was away at work she invested five dollars—most of the family's current assets—in a second-hand rowboat. It was a big gamble, but it was based on good business judgment and it paid off. The original Foss rowboat was in constant demand by fishermen and duck hunters. Mrs. Foss added to the fleet by mooring and maintaining boats at the family home in return for the privilege of renting them to cash customers who wanted to go fishing or hunting on Commencement Bay. When her husband returned from his out-of-town job he found that Thea's boat business was bringing in as much money as his carpentry.

From there on the Foss story is a maritime version of the great American fairytale come true. Thea Foss started a business with one second-hand rowboat and it developed into one of the nation's greatest towing companies, which is about as close to making a great deal out of a very little as anyone is likely to find outside a Horatio Alger novel. It's only natural that legends should be invented to add flavor to such a fine yarn.

Legend has it that Thea Foss kept her business capital in a mattress and that this mattress was the Foss Company's treasury for many years. Actually, she was a sensible business woman and she kept her money in an uptown bank.

Legend has it that when that first rowboat was acquired there was no money left to buy paint; that Mrs. Foss covered as much of it as she could with the contents of a leftover can of green paint, then finished off the job with a dab of leftover white. The big green and white Foss boats of today, according to the legend, have made a tradition out of a color scheme based on the necessity for using what was available. As a matter of fact, nobody remembers just what color that first boat *was* painted, but for many years after the Foss Company became a sizeable launch and towing fleet, its boats weren't painted green and white at all. The hulls were black, upperworks natural wood finish, funnels red and black.

These and other Foss legends make such interesting telling that it's almost a shame they aren't true, but the actual facts are quite a story in themselves.

The rowboat fleet of Thea Foss grew steadily. Sometimes she made another good buy. Arthur, the skilled carpenter, spent the time between jobs building boats. And a new generation of Foss boys was growing up to man them. Arthur, Wedell and Henry were brought up on the waterfront and were exposed early in life to boats and salt water. At first they added to their mother's problems, for she frequently had to break off her other tasks to grab for small boys whose feet were carrying them out to join their imaginations at sea; or to fish

them out when they had moved too fast for her.

By the time they were old enough to pull a pair of oars effectively their mother had probably become convinced that drowning was not a part of their destiny. Since both her sons and her cedar boats seemed unsinkable it might be practical to combine them in expanding the family business.

Foss rowboats, frequently powered by the stout arms and oars of the Foss boys, began serving the deepsea windships of the grain and lumber fleets which thronged Commencement Bay in the 80's and 90's. Sometimes the ships waited a long time in the outer harbor until there was room for them at a wharf. The sailing ships always stayed in port at least a month . . . sometimes two or three. There were many errands to be run for these waiting ships; provisions and mail to be brought aboard; messages and men to be carried between ship and shore.

There was no doubt about it. Rowboats were profitable, and Mrs. Foss set about rounding up every one in Tacoma harbor. Eventually there were more than 200 of them in the Foss fleet. It was about that time that the second engine-powered boat in the history of the Foss Company appeared on the scene. It created quite a sensation when Andrew Foss came sailing up to the landing at the helm of the S.S. *Lizzie A.*

There was considerable that could have been said about the *Lizzie A.*, and very little of it flattering. She was a diminutive stern-wheel steamboat with a number of visible weaknesses, which a clever ship carpenter could, in time, correct. She also had one major weakness which seemed to be a part of her character and was quite incurable. The little *Lizzie A.* had delusions of grandeur. She seemed to think she was really a glamorous, sleek-lined racing boat and not a beamy, modestly powered stern-wheel steamboat at all. She tried to travel like the gaily pennanted steam and naptha launches of Tacoma's playboys that slashed clean, white furrows through the blue water of Commencement Bay. The racing launches lifted their slim bows and squatted down low in the stern, and the poor little *Lizzie A.* tried to do the same. But stern-wheel steamboats can only make proper progress by reversing that process. Their bows must be down and their stern-wheels high in the water.

The *Lizzie A.*, trying to lift her stubby bows and plane, was like a fat, retired mariner with one leg trying to do acrobatic dancing. Only misfortune could result from it. Her original

THE BLUE STAR, first Foss-owned boat on Puget Sound, was powered with the engine and boiler of the wrecked steamboat **St. Patrick.**

owner, who had built her to haul dairy products down the Duwamish River, had given up trying to break her of her skittish habits, leaving her, finally, to rot on the beach. He considered her a total loss, so it was just like finding money when Andrew Foss offered him $50 for her.

Andrew repaired most of the *Lizzie A.'s* lesser defects, but no amount of alterations or ingenious cargo stowage could stop her from trying to raise her bows and plane like a racing launch. This caused her to splash and wallow and make little progress while consuming a lot of fuel in the process of accomplishing nothing. She was not a success on the Vashon Island freight run upon which Andrew embarked.

Thea Foss remained tolerant of the *Lizzie A.* up to a point, but that point was reached when it became apparent that the deluded steamboat was taking money out from instead of adding her share to the company's treasury. Only marine museums can afford to preserve ships out of sentiment. The *Lizzie A.* was losing money and Mrs. Foss wasn't running a marine museum.

She felt she must have met someone who was, however, when a stranger appeared at the landing and seemed to be admiring the steamboat, which was dozing among the row-

boats. When he proved to have cash, as well as a misguided urge to buy the *Lizzie A.*, it was obvious that he was an agent of providence, whatever his other affiliations might be. Andrew was away at the time, but this was no time for discussion . . . except as regards to the purchase price. When he returned home his steamboat was gone, but he couldn't offer much logical objection. His amazing wife had sold the *Lizzie A.* for $500 and a team of horses, and any way he figured it that was a profit of better than 1000 per cent.

The profits from the sale of the fast and commodious S.S. *Lizzie A.* (all steamboats are fast and commodious when they are up for sale) went to buy a boat which was a compromise between the rowboats and the stern-wheel steamboat. The $500 from the sale of the little stern-wheeler bought a fine little naptha launch, the *Hope.* The Foss Company was entering the second phase of its development and before long the rowboats were almost a thing of the past.

The almost forgotten breed of boats known as naptha launches was an interesting, although short-lived, product of the gay 90's. Just as the naptha launch *Hope* was a compromise in the affairs of the Foss Company, her machinery was a compromise between steam engines and

EVOLUTION—The Foss Launch and Tug Company survived many changes in fortune because its organization was flexible, a character trait which is shared by most West Coast tugboat firms. Many of the present-day diesel boats started life as nineteenth century steamboats and are still going strong after 50 years and more of hard service.

Typical of these is the present-day Foss towboat **Simon Foss,** which was launched as a Puget Sound passenger steamer at Tacoma in 1897. Converted to a steam tug in later years, but still bearing her original name, **Alice,** she worked out of Juneau, Alaska, and Olympia, Washington. Few who see her as the diesel harbor tug **Simon Foss** would recognize her as a pre-Spanish American War steamboat, but she's typical of scores of modernized old-timers in the towing fleets.

Another ship formerly named **Alice,** even older than the present **Simon Foss,** is still leading an active life under the Foss houseflag. The **Foss 18** was launched at Alameda, California, in 1892 as the steam tug **Alice.**

THE WANDERER, (right) one of the original Puget Sound Tugboat Company fleet, was one of the last active steam tugs of the Foss Company. Abandoned in 1950, her hull lies on the mudflats at the mouth of the Nisqually River on upper Puget Sound. A 128-footer, she was built at Port Blakely in 1890.

THE WALLOWA, (below) built at Portland in 1889, gained fame as a bar tug on the Columbia River before changing her name to the **Arthur Foss.** In the 1930's she underwent another purely temporary change of name, becoming the **Narcissus** while acting in the first of the "Tugboat Annie" movies.

STEAM TUG KENAI, (lower right) with diesel-powered **Wedell Foss** forward, moves a railroad car barge up Puget Sound toward the shadow of Mt. Rainier. The **Kenai,** built at San Francisco in 1904, once served as an Alaska passenger steamer. She's out of service now, but the **Wedell Foss,** formerly the government quarantine steamer **R. M. Woodward,** later the Puget Sound Tug and Barge Company's **Neptune,** is still active and a frequent winner of Puget Sound tugboat races.

gasoline engines. The naptha engine, being much simpler than a steam engine, needed no licensed engineer to operate it. It had no boiler to blow up or to utilize valuable space, and no firebox to produce the soot and ashes which were an unpleasant feature of steam launches. It worked somewhat on the principal of a steam engine, but compressed (and deodorized) naptha was released from the fuel tank to expand in the engine to a gas, which provided the

. . . AND UP SHE RISES—Offshore towboating is no job for people with queasy stomachs, as shown by these action pictures of the big **Donna Foss** working her way through ocean swells in the North Pacific. Foss tugs make voyages to Alaska, South America and across the Pacific, although three quarters of the company's business is on Puget Sound. Boats operate from three bases—at Seattle, Tacoma and Port Angeles.

working pressure. The used naptha gas was usually exhausted into condenser pipes running under the launch's hull to be led back to the fuel tank where it was put to work again.

Salesmen of the primitive gasoline engines of the 19th century could claim most of the same advantages over steam, but the naptha enthusiasts had a big point in their favor. Their engines almost always ran, whereas it was considered a minor miracle when an 1895-model gas engine consented to do anything more than squat sullenly behind its big fly-wheel and dare anybody to make it start.

After 1901, however, it was evident that the internal combustion engine was here to stay. The first gasoline launch to join the Foss fleet was the *Columbia*, which turned out so well that she was followed by a flotilla of gas boats which rivalled the old rowboat fleet. The launches brought added prosperity, for they not only serviced the big sailing ships while they lay in port, but were getting husky enough to shift them from roadstead to dock and even help them out to the straits sometimes. Each of the big windjammers meant a gross revenue of $1500 to $2000 to the Foss Company.

The launches were sometimes chartered to picnic and camping parties, as well as to police agencies for grimmer duties. Foss launches helped chase the smugglers before the cutters came to Puget Sound, and a half dozen of them were in the manhunt for the famous Western outlaw, Harry Tracy, when he commandeered a boat near Shelton in his race for freedom. But the big wind ships of the grain and lumber trade provided the bulk of Foss revenues. Those revenues increased when, early in the 20th century, it was discovered that every commercial launch in Tacoma harbor was wearing the colors of the Foss fleet. Thea and Andrew had cornered the market.

Then misfortune struck; misfortune in the form of the White Funnel Line's big bulk cargo steamer *Hyson*, which steamed up to the dock with no help from launches, pumped out her water ballast, loaded a full cargo of wheat, and was headed back to sea . . . *all inside of four days!*

Steamers had, of course, been calling at Tacoma for a long time, but they carried passengers and general cargo and high priority freight. They left the wheat and the timber to the sailing ships. It took people a little while to realize it, but that hurried visit of the *Hyson* marked the death of the beautiful sailing ships they had grown used to. Other bulk cargo steamers followed her to finish the job and, almost overnight it seemed, the great Cape Horn barks and full-rigged ships had become nothing but a memory. And the steamers provided no business for the big fleet of Foss launches.

Thea and Andrew Foss, in the face of this vast change in the economics of their business, could have concluded that their line of work had outlived its era—like the making of buggy whips, or naptha launches. They could have disposed of the fine fleet of launches that represented the faith and the hard, practical labor of two lifetimes . . . at a loss, probably, but still for enough to start over in a business that didn't need non-existent sailing ships as customers. But they didn't.

For a while, before the automobile became something more than an unreliable toy for rich men, the launches made a fair living as pleasure boats. People would charter them to go camping and picnicking, or just for an hour's ride as the wonderful climax to a holiday at Point Defiance Park. But again things changed, for suddenly the country had gone on the tin standard and people turned their backs on the lovely, placid reaches of the Sound to taste the gassy delights of the family flivver. The day of the pleasure launch was as dead as the great age of sail. While it lasted the Foss launches carried presidents, like Taft and Teddy Roosevelt, and empire builders like Jim Hill and Frederick Weyerhaeuser, but Thea and Andrew Foss knew that past glories don't pay current bills.

RUGGED POWER is typified in the lines of the 1200-horsepower **Justine Foss,** shown here in drydock. A post-war "Mikimiki" type, the **Justine** is one of the modern sea-going units of the Foss fleet. She is registered at 117 net tons.

HARBOR TUG AT WORK. The **Foss 19,** of 31 net registered tons and powered with a 200-horsepower diesel, is another of the fleet's older boats. She was built at San Francisco in 1895; was originally named the **Wigwam.**

DIVERSIFIED TASKS—At Harbor Island, Seattle, the 92-foot, thousand horsepower **Henry Foss** works a car barge in close quarters beside a Norwegian freighter while (below) the barge **Foss 98,** deeply laden with petroleum products, is towed west out of Seattle's Elliott Bay by the tug **Wallace Foss.** (Right) Wheel watch.

It was then that the company became the Foss Launch *and Tug* Company. There were log rafts and barges still to be towed on Puget Sound, and some of the huskier launches could be put to work to move them. The smaller boats, not strong enough to conform with the firm's latest change in fortunes, would have to go the way of the *Lizzie A.* In the meantime, Andrew hadn't forgotten his old trade. He began building boats of his own design, snub-nosed, husky, broad-sterned boats. They were the first specialized tugboats of the Foss fleet. The efficient *Fossberg*, built especially to turn the big sound steamers of the Black Ball Line in Tacoma's narrow west waterway was the pioneer of this class.

As this new aspect of the business grew, big steam and diesel tugs were gradually acquired —deep draft offshore huskies that could have carried the little *Lizzie A.* on their afterdecks.

Thea Foss, the indomitable woman who invested the family fortune in a second-hand rowboat in 1889 died in 1927. She had lived to see her vision and her courage pay off, for the Foss Launch and Tug Company was already a major factor in Pacific Coast water transportation.

When Andrew Foss followed her ten years later there were more ships in the fleet and many of the old steamers were being repowered with diesel engines. The Foss Launch and Tug Company had survived by keeping abreast of the times, and the power of its boats traced the development of marine propulsion. Steam and naptha, gas and diesel had powered the green and white hulls of the Foss boats. And even before that there were the husky arms of Arthur and Henry and Wedell.

The Pacific Northwest legend-builders have it that Thea Foss was the real Tugboat Annie; that *Saturday Evening Post* writer Norman Reilly Raine used her as the flesh and blood model for his nationally famous fiction character, the Grand Old Lady of the Northwest sea lanes. Realists snort at this as pure imagination, although they admit that a Foss tug, was disguised as the famed *Narcissus* to act with Marie Dressler and Wallace Beery in the film version of Tugboat Annie.

But to those who know the true story of Thea Foss and her accomplishments, the argument is unimportant. No fictional exploits, brilliant as they may be, could possibly add to the stature of the woman herself, or surpass the dreams she made come true.

ONE OF THE FOSS SEA-GOING FLEET, the **Leslie Foss,** works the bulk cargo barge **Foss 133** through the big ship lock at the Lake Washington Ship Canal in Seattle. The **Leslie,** a 1200- horse-power Mikimiki-type, was purchased from the government in 1951 to become the fifth vessel of her type in the Foss fleet.

EVENING SHADOWS AND PLACID WATERS framed the tug **Andrew Foss** in happier days, but now she rests in deep water in Grenville Channel, 135 miles south of Ketchikan, Alaska. Towing a bargeload of ore concentrates from the Polaris-Taku Mine to the Tacoma Smelter, the **Andrew Foss** was run down and sunk by the Alaska Ship Lines tug **Macloufay.** One life was lost in the sinking. The **Andrew Foss** was built at Seattle in 1905 as the U.S. Army steamer **Lt. George M. Harris.** The **Macloufay,** not seriously damaged, is a "mikimiki" type tug built at Aberdeen, Washington, in 1943. She has since been renamed **Pat rick.**

Mr. and Mrs. George Westerman and Mr. and Mrs. Bert Thompson ride a Foss boat out to watch the Maritime Day tugboat races in Seattle harbor.

Typical tugboat men Pomeroy, McWhinney, Thurston and Evans watch a boat make its landing and all agree that they could have done it more neatly.

ONE LONG—ONE SHORT

One long whistle blast, one short whistle blast; that's the signal asking for the services of the Puget Sound Tug and Barge Company of Seattle. It's a call that may be answered by any one of fifteen husky workboats, ranging in size from the 57-footers *Starling* and *Delwood* of 165 horsepower, to the 1800-horsepower, 128-foot *Wando*.

The Puget Sound Tug and Barge fleet is easily recognizable. The black-hulled tugs carry the company name on their bulwarks, topped by buff deckhouses, white pilot houses and gleaming crimson funnels with black bands at the top.

The Puget Sound fleet, like that of Foss, is a combination of big, modern deepwater boats and storied old-timers who seem bent on proving the adage that old tugboats never die. The *Goliah*, for instance, is the second oldest tugboat on active service in the Pacific Northwest. The third boat of that name in Puget Sound history, she was originally the *George W. Pride, Jr.*, built at Philadelphia in 1882. Like the other two boats which bore the name *Goliah*, she came west the hard way, around Cape Horn. The husky iron-hulled steamer arrived at San Francisco in 1886.

For many years she specialized in towing the big sailing ships through the Golden Gate, an occupation requiring fast engines and astute skippers. When word arrived from the Point Lobos lookout reporting an inbound sail, a race between rival tugs was inevitable. Both speed and trickery were employed by the competing tug masters in their efforts to get there first

and get a line aboard. The *Vigilant* usually held her own there as she is doing on Puget Sound. Well past the Biblical age of three score and ten, the latest *Goliah* is running on her third name and her second set of engines; diesels this time.

Puget Sound's *Equator* has an even more colorful past. She was launched as a windjammer back in 1888, at Benecia, California. The compact 81-foot, two-masted schooner was built for the codfishing trade, but she tasted fame and romance when Robert Louis Stevenson chartered her for the South Sea Island cruise from which he never returned.

It was on the deck of the *Equator*, under the taut canvas of full-drawing sails, that Stevenson gained the inspiration for his best remembered sea story, *The Wreckers*. There, too, he was moved to write a poem called *Aboard the Old Equator*, but that was written for the schooner's master and apparently never saw print.

Around the turn of the century the *Equator* became a steamboat. She kept her two tall masts, but bulky deckhouses and a tall funnel robbed her of the good looks that had impressed the famous writer who once sailed with her to Tahiti. Even the stout masts are gone now, and there is little of the romantic South Sea Island schooner left about the workaday diesel tug *Equator* of Seattle. But she retains her colorful past while earning her living efficiently in the

1. Since this was written, the **Goliah** and the **Equator** have made their last voyages. Supplanted by more modern boats, the iron-hulled **Goliah** went to the scrap yard; the wooden **Equator** has become part of a breakwater at Bellingham.

"ABOARD THE OLD EQUATOR," Robert Louis Stevenson made his South Sea Island cruise. Here the **Equator** is pictured as a steamer, still rigged with her original schooner masts.

(Below) The **EQUATOR** as she looked in 1955, a diesel-engined unit of the Puget Sound Tug and Barge Company fleet. She has since been scrapped.

age of the atom, which is one of the things that makes the story of the West Coast tugboats worth telling.[1]

Of course the big post-war tugs of the Puget Sound fleet have had their adventures too. The *Wando* and *Monarch* made towing history late in 1953 when they brought the newly-purchased ferries *Olympic* and *Rhododendron* on a 3000-mile voyage from Baltimore to Seattle. Captains Kelly Sprague of the *Wando* and Don Barbeau of the *Monarch* reported uneventful trips, except for the distance involved and the unusual nature of the tows they dragged along behind half a mile of wire towing cable, but things don't always work out that way.

Captain Noel Davis had the *Monarch* a year earlier, dragging a barge loaded with 26,000 gallons of aviation gasoline through a full southwest gale off the Washington coast. At the height of the storm, ten miles or so southwest of Destruction Island, the tow line broke. The laden barge went rolling and pitching off into the storm, headed for sure destruction on the rocky Washington coast. Rescue vessels,

SECOND OLDEST TUG IN THE NORTHWEST, the last **Goliah** was the third Puget Sound tug to bear that name. Built in Philadelphia in 1882, she came around Cape Horn to serve as a San Francisco Bay tug under the name **Vigilant.** Her 112-foot iron hull was powered with a 650 horsepower diesel engine.

OLD-TIMERS GET TOGETHER, as the **Goliah** (above) tows the old Puget Sound and Alaska steamer **Bellingham** through the Lake Washington Ship Canal locks to be burned as part of Seattle's annual Seafair celebration. The **Bellingham,** formerly the **Willapa** and **General Miles,** was built the same year as the **Goliah;** was the first ship of the Alaska Steamship Company. Below, in an earlier picture, the 70-year-old **Active** comes alongside the three-masted schooner **Azalea,** one of the last of the Alaska codfishing fleet. The **Active** is now the oldest vessel in the Puget Sound fleet.

summoned by the *Monarch's* radio, ended up in the lee of Tatoosh Island taking seas down their stacks while they rolled and pitched like porpoises.

While other shipping was concerned only with taking care of itself, the *Monarch,* looking more like a submarine than a tugboat, circled her runaway barge. Capt. Davis saw to it that every man on deck was wearing a life jacket and was secured by lifelines. One man was detailed as a lifeguard for every two men working. The broken tow line was cast free, a new line attached to the big towing winch aft. Then a light kedge anchor was attached to a messenger line at the end of the new hawser.

For more than eleven hours the tug stalked the storm-driven barge. Then, as the *Monarch* swept in a fast turn around the barge's plunging stern, the messenger line was flung out, the anchor hooked over the surge chain on the barge, and the tow was secured again. The crew of the *Monarch* had harpooned the runaway tank barge in much the same way men in small boats once harpooned whales.

The *Monarch* received the Bardahl Workboat Service Trophy for that job . . . an award for "outstanding navigation, seamanship and courage."

That kind of hairbreadth adventure wasn't new to the *Monarch*. A few years earlier she and the *Hercules* were assigned to tow the bombed and burned out hull of the battleship *Oklahoma* from Pearl Harbor to a San Francisco scrap yard.

It was only luck and an old-time tugboat man's trick that saved the two boats that trip.

The diesels of the *Monarch* and *Hercules* rumbled steadily as they headed across the Pacific, the dead warship surging along behind at the end of two 1400-foot cables. They had put more than 500 sea-miles astern and it was black midnight when the powerful searchlight of the *Hercules* revealed that the battleship had developed a dangerous list. The tugs radioed Honolulu for instructions; were advised to return.

Tugs and tow swung in a wide circle to retrace their course. Kelly Sprague, master of the *Hercules*, kept his searchlight playing on the *Oklahoma*. Earlier he had ordered the cable clamps on the towing engine drum loosened "just in case." Over on the *Monarch* Capt. George Anderson had done the same.

The *Oklahoma's* end came almost without warning. In Capt. Sprague's words, "She just

AN ACTIVE HARBOR TUG, Puget Sound's **Tyee** was formerly the San Francisco tug **Crowley No. 28.** An 80-footer with 450 horse-power engines, she specializes in docking ships, as shown in these pictures. Above the **Tyee** is shown working with the **Goliah** on the big **Harry Lundeberg,** later lost off the California coast. (Below) Old-time towboater John Jorgenson, serving as watchman at the Puget Sound Tug and Barge Company pier.

FLOATING POWERHOUSE, the big **Hercules** manhandles a Japanese freighter on the Seattle Waterfront. Veteran of many sea adventures, the 1200-horsepower **Hercules** is typical of the larger deepwater boats of the Puget Sound Tug and Barge Company.

MIGHTY MITE; the new harbor tugs **Titan** and **Trojan** pack 800-horsepower in their 65-foot hulls, enough to shoulder big ships into place. Here the **Titan** is shown docking a mothballed liberty ship from the Olympia, Washington, reserve fleet at a Seattle grain terminal to receive a storage cargo of surplus wheat.

NEWEST WEST COAST TUGBOAT is Puget Sound's powerful 100-foot deep-sea and harbor workhorse **Neptune,** built at Portland in 1956.

John Lee, President of Puget Sound Tug and Barge Company, holds the Bardahl Seamanship Trophy, Capt. Noel Davis holds the accompanying placque and John Haydon, Editor and Publisher of the **Marine Digest,** who has just made the presentation, looks on at the right. Capt. James Dunlap is in the foreground.

Half a ship is better than none, and these Puget Sound tugs are bringing in what's left of the wrecked tanker **Sackett's Harbor,** which had served as a floating powerhouse in Alaska. More recently the half-tanker was towed to California, where its engines were r e m o v e d to power the world's first "wine tanker" for the Petrie Wine Corporation.

LONG VOYAGE. The *Wando* moves out of Baltimore harbor with one of two ferries purchased by the Washington State Toll Bridge Authority. Astern, the **Monarch** prepares to move out on her 3000-mile voyage with the other ferry. The two ferries, renamed **Rhododendron** and **Olympic,** are now active in Puget Sound service. In 1956 the **Wando** made probably the longest non-stop tow of any American tug in history when she took the old Alaska Steamship Company liner **Alaska** from Los Angeles to Yokohama for scrapping . . . a distance of 5,480 miles.

keeled over and went down."

On the *Hercules*, Engineer Robert Freiner thought he was having a nightmare. For hours his mighty diesels had been thumping away at full towing speed. Suddenly they stopped themselves and began turning over *in reverse* at 200 revolutions a minute! The vast bulk of the *Oklahoma*, headed for the depths of the Pacific, was pulling the two tugs with her . . . so fast that water pressure had stopped their engines, then started the propellers whirling in reverse!

Solid walls of water swept over the tugs' broad sterns and across their decks. The *Monarch* was going backward at 15 knots when the unshackled cable slipped from the drum, leaving the tug still afloat. The *Hercules* passed her at far greater speed, still held in the *Oklahoma's* death-grip. In a few seconds the *Hercules* would be going under like a diving submarine, but with one big difference. The *Hercules* wouldn't be coming up again.

Captain Sprague's foresight paid off at the

last possible moment. The end of the cable whipped overboard to follow the *Oklahoma* to the still depths of the Pacific. The *Hercules* stayed pitching and rolling on the surface.

President John Lee of Puget Sound Tug and Barge Company is proud of the records his skippers and crews have made in times of peril, and he's proud of the efficient every-day useful work his crimson-stacked tugboats perform in Pacific waters. The fleet carries on the traditions of three famous names in Puget Sound towboating . . . the Cary-Davis Tug and Barge Company, Drummond Lighterage Company and Pacific Towboat Company, which were merged to form the present firm. The old-timers of the fleet, like the *Goliah* and the *Active* and the *Equator* have carried on the traditions of another age too.

And the big new tugboats of the Puget Sound fleet? They're busy making new traditions of their own.

BIG "W"

A big white "W" on a black funnel is the symbol of Seattle's Washington Tug and Barge Company, prominent on West Coast sea lanes ever since the firm was established back in 1909.

Like most of the Pacific Coast towing fleets, that of Washington Tug and Barge boasts its share of famous old time boats that have helped make maritime history for many decades. The up - to - date diesel powered *Triumph*, for instance, was once a Coos Bay, Oregon, bar tug in the days when pilot houses were considered sissified and skippers steered their craft from big sailing ship-type wheels set aft on the open deck. (A picture of the *Triumph* of that era is shown on page 14. Other pictures showing her transition from old time steamer to modern diesel are on page 45.)

The *Triumph*, built at Parkersburg, Oregon, in 1889, is the senior member of the Big W fleet, but the trim 90-footer *Reliance* has quite a history too. Built at the Cook and Lake shipyard in Ballard, the *Reliance* started life under the name *Forest T. Crosby*, in honor of a son of Captain Harry Crosby, who had founded the Washington Tug and Barge Company in 1909.

Making her maiden voyage in December, 1912, the *Crosby* specialized in towing barges between Puget Sound and British Columbia ports. During her first six months of operation she hauled 100 bargeloads of coal, brick, lumber, gravel and general freight north, towing as many as six barges at a time.

These multiple tows were pioneered by Capt. Crosby with the company's first tug, the old *Monitor*, which had once been the Puget Sound passenger steamer *Lydia Thompson*. On one of the *Monitor's* barge hauls to Canada, in January, 1911, Capt. Crosby decided to take his whole family along to celebrate, of all things, his *thirteenth* wedding anniversary.

As an old seaman, Capt. Crosby should have known better than to flout maritime superstition that way, but the weather looked fine and the barometer was high. The old *Monitor* had a festive air about her as she headed north pulling two empty scows for Boat Harbor and one loaded with brick for Vancouver. That was on a sunny Saturday.

By Sunday night the *Monitor* was bucking 50-mile an hour winds. "By Monday," Capt. Crosby reported a f t e r w a r d, "it was much worse."

"I never before saw anything in this part of the world like the weather we had. The glass went down to 28.66 at two o'clock Monday morning, and I believe that is the lowest reading we have had in these waters in a very long time." The *Monitor* came wallowing back into Elliott Bay with 20 tons of ice coating her bulwarks and deck and carrying the saddest and sickest anniversary party in Puget Sound history.

From then on, Capt. Crosby had a proper respect for that mystic number . . . thirteen.

The most famous ship to wear the Big W was the *Roosevelt*, once the Arctic exploration ship of Admiral Peary on his 1909 expedition to the

Perry Moore, well known Foss executive, was once an engineer on the **Roosevelt**.

North Pole. The *Roosevelt* was built at Bucksport, Maine, and was launched in 1905. Admiral Peary's wife christened her with the traditional bottle of champagne, but the ceremony had an unusual twist. The bottle was imbedded in a block of ice.

The *Roosevelt* was purchased by the United States government in 1915, serving as a Coast Guard vessel until 1923, when she was taken over by Washington Tug and Barge for conversion to a seagoing tug. During her towboat days, the *Roosevelt* handled many of the huge, cigar-shaped log rafts which used to be towed down the coast from the Columbia River to California ports, an operation which is described in detail in a later chapter.

The ice-scarred old *Roosevelt* was sold in 1937 to the California Towing Company. She left Puget Sound the same year, towing the big Navy collier *Jason*, bound for the East Coast. The old steamer took a severe beating from her ponderous tow, and upon arrival at the Panama Canal it seemed doubtful that she was in shape to go on with the voyage. Another tug was dispatched from New York to take over the *Jason*; the battered *Roosevelt* was eased into the old French Canal to await refitting.

She lay there a long time, her crew gradually disposing of her removable parts on the Christobal black market to obtain spending money. Finally she was abandoned where she lay. As far as is known, her old bones are still bleach-

EVOLUTION. When she was first launched as an Oregon bar tug, the **Triumph** had a minimum of deckhouse (see page 14); during her later career as a steam tug she went to the other extreme (above). Now she's a modern diesel towboat (below) with the pleasing lines of a trim twentieth century w o r k i n g g i r l. (Right) Capt. Roy Brooks and his crew aboard the **Triumph**.

FAMILY PORTRAIT: The fleet of the Washington Tug and Barge Company poses for photographer at the company's Seattle moorings. From left to right, the tugs **Bee, Triumph, Reliance, Tartar** and the petroleum carrier **General.**

Otto Johnson, senior skipper of the Washington Tug and Barge fleet, shows Churchill Griffiths, the company's general manager, a model of the tug **Reliance,** made by Capt. Johnson, who was her master for many years. (Right) Les Reynolds at the wheel of the **Reliance.** (Far right) Down in the engine room, men like Engineer Homer Troxwell keep the pulse of the tugboat beating at a healthy tempo.

ing in that tropic backwater.

James Griffiths and Sons purchased the Washington Tug and Barge Company in 1948 from Edward Jenner and associates. Churchill Griffiths is general manager of the firm. Capt. W. T. House, port captain and dispatcher and John K. Peterson, port engineer, are veteran Puget Sound tugboaters, as is Capt. Otto Johnson, the company's senior skipper. Capt. Johnson, an expert shipmodel-maker, served on the *Forest T. Crosby* in her steamboat days. After 1937, when she was rebuilt and diesel powered as the *Reliance,* he returned to her as master, a job he held continuously except during the war years when the *Reliance* served with the Navy. When the company recently added the big *Tartar* to its fleet, Capt. Johnson took over as her master.

AMERICAN OF EVERETT

Headquarters of the American Tow Boat Company is at Everett, but the units of its 21-vessel fleet get around a lot. The bright green and orange of American's tugs has added a touch of color to the Puget Sound scene for many years.

Founded in 1902 by Captain Harry Ramwell, the American Tow Boat Company has become one of the largest towing firms in the lower Puget Sound area. The present head of the company is George J. Schuchart, with Bob Van Kirk as port captain and Sid Street, chief dispatcher.

Like all the other Puget Sound towing companies, the American fleet is entirely diesel-powered nowadays, but in past years it had its share of colorful steam tugs like the *Mary C.* whose long-time master, Captain Hugh Gilmore, was one of the legendary figures of West Coast tugboating. Although only a 70-footer, the little *Mary C.* spent her early years hauling barges through the dangerous Inside Passage to Alaska.

The *Mary C.* is gone now, as is the charming little American stern-wheeler *Swinomish,* which could, until recent years, be seen trundling up and down the Snohomish River with much belching of smoke and churning of paddle-buckets. The *Swinomish* ended her days in a blaze of glory when, as "King Neptune's Flagship" at the 1956 Seattle Seafair, she was loaded with combustibles and set ablaze in Lake Washington. She thus joined other notable craft on the list of those sacrificed to Seattle's annual civic celebration . . . The *Bellingham,* once the Columbia River and Grays Harbor bar tug *General Miles* and later the first ship of the Alaska Steamship Company and Puget Sound Navigation Company, and the *Advance,* which helped make Northwest maritime history for half a century as both passenger steamer and tugboat.

Not all the old-timers are gone from the American Tow Boat Company fleet, however.

STEAM AND SAIL. Under banners of black coal-smoke, the old Pacific Towboat Company steamers **Harold C.** and **Yellow Jacket** head up the Sound with the British bark **Ganges** in tow.

MARY C. . . . an American old timer.

The famous *Mary D. Hume* is definitely an old-timer . . . the oldest in the Pacific Northwest. Built at Ellensburg, Oregon, in 1881, the *Mary D. Hume* started life as a steam brig in the coastal passenger and freight trade. She kept her auxiliary sails—square rigged foremast and schooner rigged mizzen—for a number of years, and they came in handy during the second phase of her long career. In the 1890's she went to the Far North as part of the Bering Sea whaling fleet.

That was a trade which was hard on both men and ships. When an early winter brought the solid ice in to catch the whalers above the Arctic Circle, the *Hume* was among the imprisoned ships. A number of whalers died of cold, privation and scurvy before the Revenue Cutter *Bear* came to the rescue the following spring; some of the stout whaling ships had the life squeezed out of them by the terrible press of the ice, but the *Mary D. Hume* survived.

Apparently she prospered, too. The log of Captain John Cook of the steam whaler *Bowhead* notes, "Lat. 70-36 N.; Long. 131 W. August 20, 1899, five steamers in sight. We lowered for a whale but got nothing; saw the steamer *Mary D. Hume get one. August 21st, saw the Thrasher and Mary D. Hume each take a whale."*

FACE-LIFTING FOR A WORKING GIRL . . .
Back in 1919 the American Tow Boat Company's steamer **Gwylan** provided a typical picture of a Puget Sound workboat of that era as she hugged the beach to take advantage of a favorable back-eddy. With the wind helping her along and sending the coal smoke forward from her tall stack, she could handle a long tow of logs with plenty of authority.

Lengthened, rebuilt and diesel-powered, she packs more power and operates more economically nowadays. The transformation of the **Gwylan** is typical of most of the older Northwest towboats which are survivors of the age of steam and sail. The **Gwylan** was built at Tacoma in 1902.

Shortly after the turn of the century the *Hume* was reported towing big barges—the hulks of old sailing ships mostly—between Tacoma and Alaska. On the up trips she hauled coal; on the return voyages she brought down ore for the Tacoma smelter.

The old Arctic whaler got a new lease on life a couple of years ago when she went into American's own boat yard at Everett for a complete modernization. Her ancient steam plant was replaced by a 600-horsepower heavy duty diesel and she was supplied with such new-fangled gadgets as air steering, electric towing winch, anchor winch and pumps.

Her tanks which hold 15,000 gallons of fuel oil and 3000 gallons of fresh water give her a greater cruising range than she ever had as a sea-going steamer and the big diesel has given her an unlimited future, but most of the many tugboat men who have served aboard the *Hume* were a little sorry to see the old girl go modern. Her long time skipper, Captain Frank Miller, summed it up for them when he said, "I kind of hate to see her changed; she was so quiet . . . and there wasn't any diesel smell."

But the day of the steamboat is past, as far as Northwest towboats are concerned. The *Mary D. Hume*, along with scores of other historic old craft, has received a new lease on life along with a new mode of power which makes more money, even though it may be esthetically less satisfying. The last of the steamers, the big steel-hulled *Milwaukee*, made her final voyage on the Seattle-Port Townsend car ferry run on September 17, 1955. Every active American-owned tug on Puget Sound is diesel powered now.

STERN-WHEELERS UP THE RIVER. . . .
Everett, home port of the American Tow Boat
Company, is located at the mouth of the Snohomish River, so the company operated several
stern-wheelers to bring logs down the river to
sawmills on tidewater. The 85-foot **Edison**
(right), built at Edison, Washington, in 1904,
was one of the company's early river towboats.
In 1916, tied up at an Everett dock, the **Edison**
figured in a bloody chapter of Northwest history, when I.W.W. members from Seattle attempted to land at Everett from the steamer
Verona. Gunfire from the dock and the **Edison's** decks repulsed the **Verona's** crew of
radicals, but deaths and injuries on both sides
were the tragic result of the "Everett Mas-
sacre."

THE SWINOMISH (below), a 92-foot stern-wheeler built at La Conner, Washington, in 1903, was
the last paddler in active service with the American Tow Boat Company. In 1948 she was retired
to a lakeshore moorage in Seattle as a houseboat, was set on fire as part of Seattle's 1956 Seafair
finale. Back in sailing ship days the **Swinomish** was assigned to haul a scow-load of lumber out to
an English bark in Everett harbor. The mate on the "limejuicer" looked at the **Swinomish,** belching
smoke and almost hidden by piles of lumber. Turning to the captain, he remarked, "I say, sir, this
is an odd country. They bring the sawmill out alongside the ship!"

EVERETT OLD-TIMERS. A trio of steam tugs line up for repairs at the Everett Marine Ways in pre-World War I days. The 60-foot **Grace Thurston,** left, was built at Everett in 1899, the **R. P. Elmore,** center, was launched at Astoria as a passenger steamer in 1890. The **Nellie Pearson,** right, survived to become the Washington Tug and Barge Company's diesel powered **Bee.** A 60-footer, she was built at Everett in 1900.

WAITING AT THE BOOMING GROUNDS to pick up their tows are three American Tow Boat Company steamers and two from the Pacific Tug fleet. The **Chickamauga,** left, is still working for American, while the **Active,** second from right, became a unit of the Puget Sound Tug and Barge Company when it absorbed Pacific Towboat. The **Active,** built in 1888, is one of Puget Sound's oldest active tugs.

TILLICUM. With cloud-capped mountains for a backdrop, American Tow Boat Company's **Tillicum** digs in hard to the pull of a long boom of logs on lower Puget Sound. The 87-foot **Tillicum,** built at Ballard in 1901, was originally equipped with a steam engine which developed 154 horsepower. Her present power plant is a 500 horsepower diesel.

THE STAUNCH OLD MARY D. HUME, built at Ellensburg, Oregon, in 1881, is the oldest tugboat in the Pacific Northwest. During her adventurous career she has served as a coastwise freight and passenger ship and Arctic whaler. One of the last surviving steam tugs on Puget Sound, she was recently equipped with a new diesel engine and seems destined for many more years of service.

ELLIOTT BAY TOWING COMPANY'S LOUISE II and the **Adelphus** share a tow (above). Long commanded by Capt. Marion Galligan and with numerous other members of the Galligan family in her crew, the **Louise II** is notable for the big green shamrock which graces her pilot house. The **Adelphus** has since been lost while on a voyage to Alaska.

OLD COLUMBIA BAR tug **Columbia**, which once lost her wheel and skipper in a winter storm, had a well anchored pilot house in her later years. Here she's shown assisting the disabled steam schooner **Kusko-kwim River** in Alaska waters about 1915.
... courtesy Capt. Olaf H. Hansen

Ray Quinn (right), now a well known Puget Sound pilot, once served aboard the **Neptune** which, as the **Wedell Foss,** has been a frequent winner of Northwest tugboat races.

THE NEW AND THE OLD (opposite page). The **Titan,** of the Puget Sound Tug and Barge Company, aided by the **Tyee,** takes the famous old liner **Victoria** on her last voyage as a steamship. The "Old Vic," launched in 1870 as the Cunard Liner **Parthia,** carried gold hunters to the Klondike during Gold Rush Days, made her last Alaska voyage, as a freighter, in 1952. Converted to a barge, she became **Straits 27.** In 1956, as the **Straits Maru,** she was loaded with scrap metal and towed to Japan by the deepsea tug **Sudbury** of Island Tug and Barge Company. In Japan, her last cargo removed, the "Old Vic" herself became scrap iron. The **Titan,** built in 1954, like her twin, the 1956-built **Trojan,** packs 800 horsepower in her 65-foot hull.

RICH WITH MEMORIES of another day, this classic photograph shows the little Seattle harbor tug **Trio** lying alongside the sailmaker's at Colman Dock, her decks loaded with new canvas to be delivered to an anchored windjammer in the harbor.

VETERAN TUGBOAT MAN "Kinky" Beyers at the wheel of the tug **Gleaner.**

Tugboating is a hazardous occupation, but not all the accidents are fatal. The **Reliance** was freed by the incoming tide from this embarrassing perch on a mudbank.

IMPROMPTU GET-TOGETHERS are frequent among tugboatmen when wind and weather force boats into sheltered coves or when they're "laying over for the tide." Here Capt. Rod Rossart, former skipper of the **Dolly C.,** comes aboard the **Goliah** for chow and a bit of a chat.

SEA

THE SEA AND THE WESTERN WATERWAYS have many moods and the tugboats know them all. Inward bound at sunset with the job finished and the brisk evening breeze flicking spray from the r a c i n g wake, or outward bound at dawn with the sun coming from behind the eastern hills.

MOODS

. . . to lift the mist from placid waters; miles at sea with the bow slamming through the North Pacific rollers or in a quiet roadstead where the water is a mirror for placid ships . . . the tugboats go where there is work to be done.

SEA-GOING FIRE-FIGHTER. Fireboats aren't exactly tugboats, but Seattle's first fireboat, the **Snoqualmie** (right)—which was also the first fireboat on the West Coast—was required by economy-minded city fathers to tow the city garbage scow during depression days of 1896. The big **Duwamish,** which replaced the **Snoqualmie** in 1910, has led a more dignified career. Her steam engines recently replaced by diesels, she is rated as the most powerful fireboat in the world. With her mate, the **Alki,** she lends atmosphere to a famous Seattle waterfront restaurant when she isn't fighting fires. Top and bottom pictures show the **Duwamish** in her steamer days and in her present role of motor powered fireboat.

UP SOUND

Tacoma and Olympia, sea ports on the upper reaches of Puget Sound, have been sawmill towns for generations. As such, they have seen a lot of colorful towboating. A number of the boats and men still active in the Up-Sound ports are survivors of an age when timber was loaded aboard square-riggers for the voyage 'round the Horn or piled bulwark-high on the decks of three and four masted schooners and barkentines for the coastal run to California. Some of the Up-Sound tugboat companies got their start in those days too.

Captain O. G. Olson established Tacoma's Olson Tug Boat Company back in 1891, when Commencement Bay was a haven for the deep-sea windships of every maritime nation in the world. The bright white and red boats of the Olson fleet kept busy hauling raw material to the Tacoma mills in the form of log rafts; then moving the finished product — bargeloads of sawn lumber—to the sides of the waiting ships.

Two of the old Olson steam tugs, the *Elf* and the *Olympian* are still at work on the Sound as the *Foss 15* and *Foss 16* respectively. The Olson Tug Boat Company is managed now by the son of its founder, John Olson.

Back around the turn of the century the *Elf* was skippered by Captain Biz Burnham, who had transferred along with most of his loyal and highly individualistic crew from the old stern-wheel towboat *Zephyr* when that pioneer of the Upper Sound was retired by the Tacoma Mill Company. A member of the old *Elf's* crew, known in those halcyon days as "Old Town Scotty," tells an interesting story of one voyage

which the *Elf* didn't make.

The trim little steamer had come in from Big Skookum on a Saturday evening, delivered her logs to the mill and eased across to the Olson float to tie up for the night. Most of the crew were dog-tired and turned in as soon as her lines were made fast, but the engineer and skipper went ashore. Capt. Burnham wanted to report in to the office, while the engineer felt the need for a drop of something to ward off the evening chill before retiring. The engineer stopped off at the nearest saloon. The skipper proceeded to the office, where the dispatcher met him at the door.

"Get back to the float quick, Cap'n," the dispatcher greeted him. "There's a French wheat ship in a big hurry to shift down from Seattle tonight and they're willin' to pay a premium for a fast job."

Capt. Burnham departed, having delivered himself of a few well-chosen sentiments regarding frog-consuming bounty-earners who kept honest tugboat men from getting a decent night's sleep.

The *Elf* lay snoring at the landing float to the gentle tune of escaping steam, but there was a light in the galley. Old Town Scotty was setting out a pan of rolls, neatly wrapped in one of the assistant engineer's old undershirts, to rise for breakfast baking.

"Belay the baking!" commanded the *Elf's* master. "Get to the saloon quick and bring back the engineer. We got a job." Scotty wasted no time heading shoreward. Capt. Burnham went below to get the fireman out of his bunk and

ALONG TACOMA'S WATERFRONT, the Olson Tug Boat Company fleet poses for its picture on a quiet day in 1909. The rival Tacoma Tug and Barge Company's **Favorite** managed to sneak into the picture too, just astern of the **Echo.** The **Elf,** with a fine head of steam in her boiler, appears ready to tow her two fleet-mates, **Olympian** and **Echo,** back to their moorings once the shutter has clicked.

OLSON TUG BOAT COMPANY'S MADRONA was the scene of both a wedding and a twenty-fifth anniversary observance on the part of Capt. and Mrs. Art Torgesen. The 55-foot **Madrona,** built at Tacoma in 1923, was skippered by Capt. Torgesen during most of her service on the Upper Sound.

awaken the dreaming deck hands.

Within twenty minutes the *Elf's* boiler pressure had the safety valve popping and the deck hands were standing by the lines, but neither Scotty nor the engineer had returned. The skipper knew it was only a five minute stroll to the engineer's favorite saloon. He sent one of the deck hands to see what had happened. Twenty minutes later he sent the other deck hand. Impatient, he dispatched the fireman on their trail after a lapse of fifteen minutes. The fireman didn't come back either. Talking to himself, Capt. Burnham went to wake up the mate. After that he had the *Elf* all to himself. The rest of the crew was out looking for the engineer.

A half hour after the mate's departure, the skipper sorrowfully watched Tacoma Tug and Barge Company's *Fairfield* steam by toward Elliott Bay and the waiting grain ship.

"A crew the likes of mine would drive a man to drink," he muttered darkly to himself. Then, brightening somewhat at the thought, he clambered over the bulwark of the lonely *Elf* and set a course for the hospitably glowing lights of the saloon on the hill.

THE MANZANITA was built in 1899 as the **North Star,** serving for many years as a cannery tender and fishing steamer in Alaskan waters. Now rejuvenated with a powerful diesel engine, she spends most of her time towing logs for the Olson Tug Boat Company. Her roomy cabin and foc'sle make her popular with her crew and are reminders of the days when she carried crews of twenty men and more to the northern fishing banks.

The *Fairfield*, which took that night's towing job away from the crewless *Elf*, is another old-timer that's still active on the Upper Sound. The *Fairfield* was a product of the Crawford and Reid yard in Old Tacoma, where many a fine tugboat was built. She came out in 1898, constructed for the Tacoma Tug and Barge Company with Robert McCullough and Captain T. S. Burley composing the firm. A pretty and rakish little craft, she was originally powered with a fore and aft compound engine and Scotch marine boiler and could, in the words of the Tacoma *News-Tribune's* Marine Editor, Jim Bashford, "run like the proverbial scared wolf."

The *Fairfield* was active in many dramatic

THE JAUNTY FAIRFIELD has worked for Tacoma Tug and Barge Company since her launching at the Crawford and Reid Yard in 1899. She was a training ship for a score of well known Puget Sound masters and engineers, among them Capt. Fred Sutter who, on the passenger steamer **Magnolia,** gained fame as a racing skipper in memorable battles with Capt. Chance Wyman of the **Vashon.** (Below) Capt. Fred Sutter.

events around Tacoma's harbor. There was the mysterious sinking of the British sailing ship *Andelana,* with the loss of all hands, and the *Fairfield* searching for the wreckage. There was the big bark *Sir Robert Fernie* adrift in an evening gale and swept toward the beach at Brown's Point until the little *Fairfield* went tearing across the bay under a cloud of coal smoke to get a line aboard. Then she hung on like a bulldog to keep the big Cape-Horner in deep water.

There was the time, too, when a gravel scow alongside the *Fairfield* dumped its load suddenly, dipping far under water, then rising to impale the tug on its deck posts. That was almost curtains for the *Fairfield,* but she managed to beach herself before she sank. Now she's diesel-powered, like the rest of the Puget Sound towing fleet, but in her day she served as training ship for such famous marine steam engineers as Oscar Lorenz, Robert McDowell, Walter McCullough, George Kingsbury, Ally McDowell, Wynn Williams, Walter Sutter, Percy and Miles Coffman, Reuben Shade, Frank Pillow, Billy Allison, Jesse Murry, Frank Watson and Joe Allen.

Her list of skippers, too, sounds like an Upper Sound maritime hall of fame. Besides Burnham, there were Billy Phillips, Clarence Wirts,

PRIDE OF THE CAPITAL CITY TUGBOAT COMPANY fleet at Percival's Dock, Olympia, in 1928. The **Edward A. Young,** left, was just beginning her career as one of the first new diesel tugs on Puget Sound. The **Prospector,** built in 1898, was soon to end hers. One of the Northwest's last wood-burners, she was retired in 1930, burned on the beach soon afterward. The **Edward A. Young** is now part of the Tacoma Tug and Barge Company fleet.

"OLD-TIMER," cook on the **Edward A. Young,** takes his ease outside the galley at Capital City Tug moorings in Olympia. **Virjo Young** and **Mizpah** in the background.

THE SANDMAN looked more like a yacht than a tug in 1910 when she posed at Olympia, along with the stern-wheelers **S. G. Simpson, Greyhound** and **Multnomah.** Her heavy-duty gas engine was a featured display at Seattle's Alaska-Yukon-Pacific Exposition of 1909.

THE DOCTOR, above, and the E. G. English, below, started life as passenger steamers on Upper Puget Sound. The Doctor once carried passengers and freight between Olympia and Kamilche, while the English, as the stern-wheeler S. G. Simpson, gained fame on the Olympia-Shelton run. The Doctor was later a unit of the Stevenson & Blekum towing fleet in Seattle, while the E. G. English ended her days towing log rafts from the mouth of the Skagit River to Camano Island.

Veteran towboaters get together as Engineer Nick Burnham, Captain Biz Burnham and Dr. G. A. Stansfield (Old Town Scotty) meet to talk over old times on the stern-wheeler Zephyr and the tug Elf.

Sid Burley, Arthur Thompson, Frank Winchester, Vince Libo, Fred Sutter, "Zoo" Murry, Oscar Gates, Jack Schroll, Gage Wheeler, Henry Chapin, Charley Berg, Frank Hofbaurer and many others.

Puget Sound's first tug, the *Resolute*, chose the Upper Sound as the place in which to blow herself up, and strange things have been happening in those waters ever since. Like the time the Foss launch *La Thea*, carrying the mail from Seattle to Tacoma, broke a gear and would only run in reverse. Skipper Charlie Geddes and deck hand Bill Case, later a Foss dispatcher in Tacoma, knew that the mail must go through, so they took her to Tacoma backwards at a good eight knots, to the intense astonishment of all hands aboard the Seattle-Tacoma passenger steamers.

One passenger on the *Indianapolis*, a dignified, fat gentleman with a cane, leaped onto a lifeboat and wildly motioned with his cane, trying to make Capt. Geddes understand that he should turn his craft around and proceed sharp end forward.

The *Fossberg* met the *La Thea* along the way to pick up the mail, but the *La Thea* made it all the way to Tacoma in four hours travelling like an Oozelfinch . . . that fabled bird which doesn't care where it is going, being interested only in where it has been.

Later this confusion spread to the Foss office, when a dispatcher on duty on a chill and foggy night kept hearing ships whistling for Foss tugs—two long and two short blasts of their steam whistles. He couldn't locate the ships which were doing the calling, which is no great mystery, once it's explained. A steam radiator in the Foss office had sprung a leak and was emitting jets of steam on varying notes of the musical scale, but always on the same tempo . . . two longs, two shorts.

More recently, Captain Elmer Edwards and Mate Everett McVickers of the *Carl Foss*, shortly after passing the federal penitentiary on McNeil Island, noted that they had a strange passenger with them. The stranger, poorly dressed for the occasion in underwear and hat, was shivering on the log boom astern. Fortunately, deck hand Scotty Huntley had a pistol, although there were no bullets for it and the firing pin was missing. It was sufficient, however, to intimidate the boom rider, once the *Carl Foss* had been stopped and many fathoms of towing cable reeled in to bring her alongside the tow. The *Carl Foss* radioed the *Peter Foss* in Tacoma. Dispatcher Bill Case picked up the

HOMEWARD BOUND

LOG BOOMS AND BARGES are hard work for tugboats, but a great convenience for sea gulls, who like to hitch rides on them. These are cruising Puget Sound on the barge **William Nottingham.**

conversation on the tugboat band and called the penitentiary by telephone. Shortly thereafter a couple of fast prison boats converged on the *Carl Foss* to relieve the crew of their chilled guest.

The escaped convict was returned to the warmth and comfort of McNeil Island and there was talk of a reward for the crew of the *Carl Foss*. So far, according to McVickers, they haven't seen it.

Even the sound of wedding bells has been heard on Up Sound tugs. Captain Art Torgesen, 27-year veteran with Olson Tug Boat Company, found himself in love with both the girl of his choice and his handsome tugboat, *Madrona* at one stage of his career, so he compromised. Capt. and Mrs. Torgesen became man and wife on the *Madrona's* deck, with the minister using a pair of bitts for a pulpit and the overflow of wedding guests bobbing alongside in other Olson tugs.

Twenty-five years afterward, while skippering the old Olson tug *Capt. O. G. Olson*, renamed *Karen* and hauling logs for the Campbell Towing Company in Wrangell, Alaska, Capt. Torgesen spotted the *Madrona* moored in Ketchikan. He summoned his wife and they celebrated their twenty-fifth wedding anniversary drinking coffee in the galley of the tug aboard which they were married.

It takes an able and determined man to retain control over the same tugboat and the same woman for twenty-five years, but there has always been the stuff of heroes in those tugboat men of the Upper Sound. This excerpt from the Tacoma *Ledger* of December 5, 1904, tells, in the stirring prose of its Marine Editor, its own story:

"YOUNG NAVIGATORS SAVE MAN'S LIFE

"Two juvenile navigators, each aged 13 years, saved a man from drowning at the Flyer *dock last evening about 7 o'clock while a crowd of excited men on the wharf yelled themselves hoarse shouting directions and encouragement. For all their noise the man would probably have drowned if the boys hadn't happened along, for he had been in the cold water for 15 minutes and was too exhausted to scarcely make another effort toward keeping afloat.*

"The young heroes of the adventure are Henry Foss, son of the proprietor of the Foss boathouse, and Willie Todd, a son of Glen Todd, proprietor of the Commercial Dock store. They had been over to Quartermaster Harbor in the launch Hope *and on coming abreast of the*

Flyer *dock were attracted by the shouts of the men on the dock.*

"The boys put the wheel hard over and went in across the course of the Flyer, *which was rapidly approaching. They reached the half drowned man, but found their strength taxed to the utmost to get him into the launch. He was too full of water to help himself and the boys were not strong enough to lift him over the gunwale.*

"In order to get out of the way of the incoming steamer they concluded to tow him to the landing, but just before they started, with a heave all together, they managed to hoist the heavy body of the man aboard. There was just time left to dodge the Flyer, *but the young seamen were equal to the occasion and shortly had their man safely at the boathouse."*

The "juvenile navigator' of the launch *Hope* is grown up now, an admiral in the U.S. Naval Reserve and president of the Foss Launch and Tug Company.

TUGBOAT CREW. Men of the Alaska Freight Line's tug **Macloufay** line the rail before their ship heads north on a routine voyage to Alaska. The **Macloufay,** now renamed **Patrick,** has probably made as many round trips between Puget Sound and Alaska as any vessel in recent maritime history. In August, 1956, Alaska Freight Lines' port captain, M. A. "Doc" Stream, tallied up the voyages made by the line's eight tugs regularly in that service. He came up with these totals:

Patrick completing her 102nd trip, **Shinn** her 100th trip and **Michael,** 91st trip. Other boats in the running were, **Kelly,** 83 trips, **William,** 61, **Martin** 62, **Earnest,** 57, and **Charles,** 45.

The **Patrick's** 100th voyage was also the 100th for her young skipper, Captain Ray Thurston, who took command of the big tug in 1949. Three other crew members also joined the century club that voyage: Chief Engineer Richard Goldsmith, Assistant Engineer Lawrence E. McGuire and Seaman James A. Rawhauser.

PORTLAND STERN-WHEELERS Hercules and Cascades help the Sarah Dixon work a giant log raft downstream, where an ocean-going tug will take over for the long—and perilous—voyage to California.

TOTE THAT RAFT

Back in the mid-1890's an East coast lumber-man named Joggins had an idea. Watching the little wooden lumber schooners struggle to take on full timber cargoes that totalled only a few hundred thousand board feet, it seemed to him that a lot of time and money was being wasted. Since lumber floats nicely by itself without being put in ships, why not dispense with the ships and send the lumber to market supported by its own buoyancy instead of by expensive chartered bottoms?

After due cogitation and experimentation, he came up with a design which he felt would put his theory into practice. Known as the "Joggins Raft," his brain child has survived to this day with variations and changes in name. In effect, it was simply a huge, cigar shaped boat constructed of logs chained together to form a solid, hull-shaped mass of timber. In this manner, several million board feet of timber could be hauled off to market by a single tug doing

the work of a whole fleet of lumber schooners. That was the theory, anyway.

Out on the West Coast lumbermen and ship owners kept a close watch on the progress of the much publicized Joggins raft. Shipping men were not enthusiastic, for it was freely predicted by supporters of the raft idea that its success spelled the end of the coastal lumber fleets. Loggers felt differently about it. As a cheap and efficient method of getting their product to the California market it could mean added profits for them.

So the news of the first raft's failure was greeted with mixed reactions in the Northwest. The maritime fraternity went around happily saying, "We told you so," when word arrived that the raft had been battered to pieces and strewn along the Atlantic coast long before it reached its destination. Logging operators were saddened for a while, but they brightened up somewhat when it was learned that smaller versions of the original giant made it to port in later efforts. This news was so encouraging that it was decided to build a West Coast ver-

CAPTAIN ROBERTS OF THE RANGER had one of the most frustrating experiences in tow-boating history when he tried to move the first big log raft from Coos Bay out to sea, back in 1893. Like many of the old time sea-going tugs, the Ranger was steered by a sailing ship-type wheel and the pilot enjoyed plenty of fresh air.

sion of the Joggins raft.

The project got under way on Coos Bay in 1893, and it took most of the summer and early fall to raft in the thousands of big logs needed and to lash them into the massive wooden cigar the specifications called for. It contained nearly 5,000,000 board feet, which is a great deal of timber, and although most of it was out of sight under water, the giant raft was an impressive sight as it floated off Marshfield waiting for a tug to pick it up.

It was November when the raft was ready to go, and November is not the most pleasant month of the year for offshore tugboating. Captain Roberts of the steam tug *Ranger*, selected to haul the raft to California, probably expected some trouble when he cast a practiced eye first on his monstrous tow and then on the black clouds out off the bar. But he didn't expect quite as much trouble as he was destined to have. If he had, he would surely have sold out his interest in the *Ranger*, and gone to farming.

Tug and tow pulled away from Marshfield in the midst of a sad November drizzle. Captain Roberts planned to work down the bay, getting the feel of his tow, while it was still more or less daylight, but he had no intention of trying to cross the bar without a stopover. He figured on arriving at Empire City, just inside the jetty, during low tide, so he planned to tie up

at the dock there to wait for the flood before attempting the tricky bar crossing.

Unfortunately, Captain Roberts had n e v e r tried to make contact with a dock during an ebb tide with five million board feet of pure cussedness veering and wallowing and taking over control of his tug. Missing the wharf, both tug and raft went careening down the bay toward the bar, where the water was low and the surf high. Bellowing through the engine room voice tube for more steam, keeping a sharp eye out for helpful eddies, and spinning the wheel hard over, the unfortunate skipper managed to ram tug and tow hard ashore, safe inside the bar, but high and dry on an ebbing tide. So ended the first episode of this melancholy drama.

At high tide that night Captain Roberts, having exhausted his vocabulary completely, went silently to work to get things under way again. At the height of his effort the *Ranger* rammed against the wallowing raft, smashing her rudder and making herself as unmanageable as the unmentionable tow she had been fighting with all day and half the night. It took two days to get the rudder working again.

At the end of this frustrating period Roberts decided to get the hell out of Coos Bay with no more fooling around. Trying to get his Joggins raft over the Coos Bay bar was making him

feel a little like the Flying Dutchman spending all eternity trying to round the Cape of Good Hope. Crowding on a full head of steam, black coal smoke belching from her tall stack, safety valve popping, the sturdy *Ranger* took over the pesky raft with a strong hand, yanking it down the bay toward the bar before it could take over again. Then the *Ranger's* engine broke down.

Four days later, with engine repairs completed, Captain Roberts jangled the engine room gong to get under way again. There was no use fooling with the voice tube; he and the engineer weren't speaking to each other.

This time the *Ranger's* mechanism functioned perfectly. The engine was still turning over smoothly when the raft took a sudden sheer to pile up uncompromisingly on the beach. The echo of a faint but unpleasant snicker was wafted through the speaking tube from engine room to helm.

Another 24 hours of sweat, toil and epic profanity saw the timber monster afloat again, but not for long. Before the tug could get things under control the raft had grounded again; further out to sea this time and in a dangerously exposed position on the bar's south spit. The unfortunate tug kept a strain on the towing hawser all night hoping to dislodge the devilish raft when the tide rose. She kept her bulldog grip even after a nasty storm came up to send breakers crashing clear across the stranded raft. The *Ranger's* stubbornness was rewarded, in a way, when the tow suddenly came off the beach at one o'clock in the morning. But the raft still refused to take orders from the tug.

It went careening out over the bar, the poor *Ranger* bucketing along behind until somebody cut the tow line.

Captain Roberts, speechless again by now, headed out to sea to ride out the storm and wait for daylight. Passing back over the bar at dawn, he spotted the raft on the beach again, piled up on the north side of the jetty a half mile or so from where it had been the night before.

Three more days and nights saw the thing afloat again, but again it took charge of things . . . and again poor Roberts had to run his tug ashore to keep from being hauled out to sea bodily. There was a regular hurricane screaming outside the bar by this time, so when the mess was afloat again the skipper decided to return to Empire City and have another try at the wharf. On the way the raft went off on another ramble, ending up hard and fast on the middle quicksands. Captain Roberts knew when he was licked. He sent for the tug *Liberty* to help him, and after the two boats had worked hard for five days the raft floated off the sands all by itself. On December 2 it was tied up at Empire City again.

By this time the head office had come to the belated conclusion that the *Ranger* probably wasn't quite powerful enough to handle the raft under all conditions. A larger steamer, the *National City*, was dispatched to take over the job. to the intense delight of Captain Roberts and the entire crew of the *Ranger*.

The big *National City* grabbed the monster raft by the nose on December 16, bulldozing it across the bar before it had time to engage in

CONTAINING ENOUGH TIMBER to build a small city, one of the giant sea-going log rafts waits for tugs to move it down the Columbia River for its coastwise voyage to California.

any further deviltry. With a prideful blast or two of her whistle, the *National City* squared away for the southward run down the coast.

Six days later she met a gale off Cape Mendocino. The Joggins raft fell apart like a pack of cards, strewing its five million feet of logs untidily along the Northern California coast. There was no gathering up the pieces this time, and the first attempt at building a sea-going log raft on the West Coast was written off as a flat failure. The only bright spot in the whole thing was the fact that lumber was much cheaper in those days than it is now, and the raft owners didn't even have that knowledge to cheer them.

Such a fiasco might have discouraged a less hardy breed than the Northwest loggers, but being gamblers at heart, which is one of the prerequisites for being a logger, it wasn't long until they were trying again.

The second Big Raft was assembled on the Columbia, 40 miles up-river from Astoria on the Oregon shore. It looked much like the first one, was built in a cradle and chained together out of some 10,000 big Douglas fir logs. When completed, with cradle removed, the monster was 525 feet long and while it had only seven feet of freeboard at its highest point above the water, its draft was close to 20 feet. Like an iceberg, most of its bulk was under water. A huge, cigar-shaped cylinder, it had a circumference of 137 feet at the center, tapering to a 60-foot circumference at each end. It contained

about 5,000,000 feet of lumber.

The main chain, running the full length of the raft, was the two-inch iron anchor chain of an ill-fated sailing ship named *Vandalia*, which had stranded years before with considerable loss of life. Iron cross chains, nearly as heavy as the old ship's anchor cable, were wrapped all the way around the cylinder at 12-foot intervals. They were so attached to the main chain that the strain of towing would be evenly distributed to all points of the raft.

The finished product looked as seaworthy as a whale and a good deal bigger, but it was destined for the same sad fate as the first one. The big San Francisco tug *Monarch* put her hawser on the raft on October 12, 1894, and, the bar being temporarily cooperative, yanked her unwieldy tow out to sea with little difficulty. By midnight, however, the s i t u a t i o n had changed, for a 40-mile gale was sweeping up the c o a s t from the southeast. Bucking the storm, the *Monarch* was slowed to a bare crawl; then, as the wind and seas grew, there was no progress at all. By 4 o'clock in the morning the tug had made less than 18 miles headway from the bar. The gale subsided somewhat at dawn and slow progress down the coast was resumed.

An even worse storm swept in the second evening. All night long the tug and the huge raft wallowed in the trough of the sea while the great logs groaned and creaked against the restraining chains. The wind eased up again the following morning, but the sea remained

BIG CIGAR. The sea-going log rafts were lashed together with tons of ponderous metal chain, but North Pacific storms took frequent toll, scattering the millions of feet of logs along the Oregon and California coasts in wasteful abandon. (Photo from University of Oregon)

violent, and dawn brought an unpleasant disclosure to the tug's crew. Logs were smashing their way out of the big cigar fore and aft, and it was evident that the thing was about to come apart at the seams. At 10 o'clock that morning (October 14) the tug's skipper estimated that 46 miles had been made from the mouth of the Columbia River. He kept going down the coast, barely making steerage way and watching the stray logs pop out of the great bundle astern. This was unpleasant enough, but even nastier weather was ahead.

The morning of October 15 found the *Monarch* hooting her slow way through a cold, dripping fog. The tug was rolling violently in a heavy westerly swell and her crew could only guess what was happening to the raft, for it

was hidden in the fog. That afternoon the fog was driven away by a new gale. Forty mile an hour winds whipped up an ugly cross sea to tear at the weakening raft. This went on all night and it was obvious at the next dawn that the logs would never reach the California mills. Only 75 feet of the once great hulk remained attached to the hawser and that was diminishing rapidly.

When the last of the logs had dropped out to go wandering off in the storm the 60 tons of iron chain was all that was left of the second Big Raft. The chains, still attached to the towing hawser, promptly sank, anchoring the *Monarch* securely. The hawser had to be cut to release the tug, which left nothing at all of the Oregon loggers' ambitious project. The *Van-*

dalia's anchor chain had joined its ship again in Davy Jones' Locker.

Coastal sailors said this second fiasco was just what might have been expected. In the first place the giant rafts, which would rob thousands of honest seamen of jobs if they were successful, were contrary to nature; monstrosities which might be good newspaper copy but could hardly be expected to stand up to North Pacific storms. In the second place, nobody but a plain fool would use such an unlucky object as the anchor chain of a lost ship to wrap the danged thing up with in the first place. That was tempting ocean providence.

Logging operators, outraged at the thought of millions of feet of their valuable timber being scattered to the tender mercies of beachcombers, muttered darkly of other factors. The Pacific Coast seamen's unions, just getting a foothold in those days, were viewed by capitalists with about as much enthusiasm as was the I. W. W. in later years. The seamen, long considered fair game for the violence of crimps and ships' officers, were accused now of using violent methods in looking out for their own welfare. There were those who felt that if providence was being tempted it was because coastal seamen were entrusted with the big rafts that were designed to put most of them out of work. There were even some who went so far as to say right out that the raft chains were only partly loosened by the sea; that the preliminary work had been performed by the brethren of the seamen's union.

Whatever the facts in the case may be, a third Joggins raft did manage to crawl through the Golden Gate on August 1, 1895. The successful raft, built at the same point on the Columbia River as the second one, was an almost exact counterpart of the earlier ones that didn't make it. It was bigger than the others — it packed more than 7,000,000 feet of lumber inside its huge iron chain lashings—but it was the same old cylindrical timber cigar advocated by Joggins.

Stern-wheel towboats brought it down the river to Astoria, shouldering it along from the sides as if it were a huge ship. Off Astoria the tow line was transferred to the bar tug *Relief*, which hauled it offshore where the steam collier *Mineola* was waiting to take over the rest of the job.

The *Mineola* headed south, the raft trailing far astern at the end of 500 feet of chain and 1200 feet of heavy manila line. The Pacific, for the first time, cooperated with the tug and tow.

It was calm and placid when the *Mineola* took over the raft, and it stayed that way for the whole voyage. The raft was better than 100 miles closer to its destination by the end of the first 24 hours. The *Mineola* steamed down the coast at a steady 4½ knots, the Big Raft trailing behind as docilely as a well trained puppy.

There was a long-delayed celebration in Northwest logging circles when the monster arrived safe in San Francisco Bay without a log missing. Gloom was thick around the coastal shipping offices, at the union halls and aboard the steam schooners and sailing droughers of the West coast lumber fleet, but it lifted when no immediate effects were felt. The Big Raft had made it, but people remembered the expensive failures. Most shippers preferred to

TUGBOAT TRANSFORMATIONS aren't confined to Puget Sound and British Columbia waters. The passenger steamer **Reliable** (above) was a changed lady when she became a river tug (below).

BEAM SEA. The wind was whipping coal smoke from her tall stack and the sea was kicking up white as the old Cary-Davis steamer **Katahdin** edged in toward the lee of a waiting barge and the cook peeked out the galley door to see how things were going. The **Katahdin,** built at Seattle in 1899 wouldn't be recognized by her old cook if he could see her now. As the **Catherine Foss** she's another of the old-timers rejuvenated with a diesel engine.

trust to the familiar hazards of the lumber schooners, and the sea-going rafts failed to reduce the "Scandinavian Navy" of the lumber ports to any noticeable degree.

Davis rafts and other variations of the original Joggins design were dispatched from Pacific Northwest ports for San Francisco at intervals in the years that followed. Some made it, some didn't. Sea-going log rafts are still in use, although seldom seen now on the coastwise route to California. They are used widely to haul logs down from Alaska and northern British Columbia camps in bulk. Further south, the big rafts are broken up to form conventional flat booms for dispatch to sawmills and paper plants.

BRITISH COLUMBIA

The Canadian Pacific Northwest province of British Columbia is booming with growth and energy, and is, in the process, building up one of the world's largest and finest tugboat fleets. So far the supply of boats has not been able to keep up with the demand of cargo to be towed. New industries springing up along the coast are providing employment for anything with enough buoyancy to float and enough power to pull a string of logs or a loaded barge.

As a result, some of the Canadian tugs in regular use aren't as up-to-date as their sisters south of the border. Some of them have been hurriedly converted from o t h e r trades, fish packing and cannery tending, and such, to enter the towing field. But big, modern tugs are being added to the British Columbia towing fleets almost daily. Some of them are strikingly handsome little ships, and the Canadian tugboat register presents interesting extremes, from old steamers, of which there are many left, to sleek, streamlined diesels of the most advanced design.

British Columbia is pointing the way in tugboat development today just as it did 70 years ago. The difference is that the powerful, modern boats of the 1950's have plenty of jobs to keep them busy and pay their bills. When the Northwest's first super-tug went into service there in the 1880's the region's economy hadn't grown up to her size, so she was an economic failure.

This historic craft was the *Alexander,* a veritable giant of a tug designed to operate either on inland waters or well out at sea. She was a side-wheel steamer with a low, long hull and two tall, raked funnels fore and aft of her wheels. She looked a lot like the huge side-wheel towboats that still pull their long strings of barges on the Rhine River of Germany. Her advent was hailed with patriotic fervor, for she put the biggest American tugs of that day to shame, but she found little business. Most of the towing jobs could be handled by smaller boats—at much less cost. The expensive *Alexander* had a brief and unprofitable career, but she was a distant forerunner of things to come.

Early day British Columbia tugboats didn't have only superior size and power to boast about, either. Some of them had careers of wild adventure that rivalled the tallest tales that could be spun on the American side of the boundary line. The old *Goliah* may have been a pirate, from a technical viewpoint, but she was never as bloody a pirate as the Canadian *Forward.*

The *Forward* spent most of her life as a gunboat, plodding up and down the British Columbia coast in support of law and order. The Haida Indians respected her cannon and gave her a wide berth, so her naval career was uneventful . By 1869 she was getting a bit old and creaky, so was decommissioned to be sold at auction in Victoria.

It was assumed that, in civilian life, she would take up a respectable life as a tower of logs. Her new owners, in fact, assured the representatives of the Canadian government that this was exactly what they had in mind for her.

Down on Puget Sound the mill tug *Polit-*

MIGHTY SIDE-WHEEL TUG ALEXANDER was ahead of her time and consequently lost money, but today British Columbia towing companies are busy building more and more powerful boats to move the constantly increasing tonnage of Canadian water-born commerce.

kofsky was considered quite stylish with her battery of Russian cannon, so nobody thought it unreasonable for the tugboat *Forward* to keep *her* shiny muzzle-loaders. But the *Forward* never towed a single log. Her new owners wanted quicker profits, and they got them from a suave San Salvadorian named Pedro Viscayno. He informed them that he was a representative of the Navy of San Salvadore, which was looking for just such a fine gunboat as the *Forward*. As Senor Viscayno was prepared to make a cash deal—in gold—he had himself a ship.

SEA-GOING TUG HARO specialized in moving big sailing ships to the Hastings Lumber Company dock in Vancouver. Lumber products are still the basis of most British Columbia tugs' payloads.

The Republic of San Salvadore may have bought the well-armed "tugboat" with public funds for legitimate purposes, but Senor Viscayno, convinced that possession is nine points of the law, also had visions of quick profits. And he had the *Forward*.

As the first step toward wealth and power, Viscayno personally declared war on Mexico, although he failed to notify that sovereign power of his action. The first the disturbed Mexican government knew about it was when word was received that the *Forward* had waddled down the coast to bombard the city of Guaymas. Viscayno and his merry men had then shot, raped, and looted their way through the town, confiscated a couple of Mexican coasters, the *San Pablo* and *Colima*, to help carry their ill-gotten gains and proceeded down the coast.

Mexico, having no naval vessels capable of engaging the pirate in battle, called loudly for help from Great Britain and the United States. Authorities at Victoria were shocked to learn that their *Forward*, which they had assumed to be off somewhere towing logs, was actually down south terrorizing a friendly power, and wasted no time in dispatching ships of war in pursuit.

The United States felt a little guilty, too, the *Forward* having been sold and outfitted for her

CANADIAN VETERANS. Part of the Pacific Coyle Navigation Company fleet of 30 years ago is pictured here. Powerful tugs of Canada's "Red Band Fleet" have been part of the Northwest maritime scene for many years. The company presently operates a fleet of 15 vessels. J. D. Coyle is president and general manager of the firm. George Reid is dispatcher for the towing fleet.

villianous career in San Francisco, so the *U. S. S. Mohican* was also sent out on her trail. The American gunboat caught up with the pirate craft near the mouth of the Teacapan River. The *Forward's* piratical master, not liking the *Mohican's* business-like appearance and grinning gun-ports, promptly ran his flagship up the shallow river.

The *Mohican's* draft was too great to allow her to follow, but she didn't give up the chase. A detachment of 88 seamen and marines under a Lieutenant Bronson were told off to man the small boats. In short order the little flotilla of six boats was slashing up the river in the pirate's wake. The lead boat mounted a 12-pounder howitzer, but the expedition's success depended mostly on the cutlasses of the seamen and the muskets of the marines.

Forty miles upstream they came upon the poor old *Forward*, aground on a sandbar and listing drunkenly. They were greeted by a scattering of shots from the wrecked steamer, but most of the pirates were manning a hastily constructed shore battery armed with the best of the *Forward's* guns.

The landing party stormed the pirate fort, answering cannon fire with musket balls. After firing a few salvos, which left an American ensign and coxswain dead, and six men wounded, the pirate crew made a strategic withdrawal. As far as is known, they may still be running.

After rolling the abandoned cannon into the river, the survivors of the Navy expedition turned their attention to the unfortunate *Forward*. After removing six chastened pirates from her decks, they smashed her engines and set fire to her. The six members of her erstwhile crew were duly turned over to the tender mercies of the Mexican government. History doesn't record their ultimate fate, but there is little doubt that it was highly unpleasant.

As for the *S. S. Forward*, she was reduced to charred timbers and rusty iron on the backwaters of a little Mexican river, proving that crime does not pay, even for steamboats. Log towing is less glamorous than piracy, perhaps, but the old gunboat would have done better to have pursued the legitimate trade she was intended for.

A lot of fine big Canadian tugboats are doing well at log hauling nowadays, for the timber and paper-making industries of British Columbia are growing fast and have tremendous appetites.

79

ISLAND TUG AND BARGE

The Island Tug and Barge Company of Victoria, probably the largest towing firm in Canada, got its modest start in that business in 1925. It started when Harold Elworthy quit his job with the British Columbia Salvage Company. He had a little over a hundred dollars in cash and a driving ambition to own a tugboat of his own.

His ambition was realized, with the help of a sizeable bank loan, when he took over the little tug *Quinsita*, renaming it *Island Planet*. This was the Island Tug and Barge Company in 1925, and its first job was the towing of a boom of logs to Victoria for a $125 fee. A lot of logs have been towed to the mills by Island boats since then.

The company towed the first big Davis rafts from Nootka Sound to mainland processing

COMPLETING THE LONGEST single-line deep-sea towing operation in marine history, the **Sudbury** and **Island Sovereign** arrive at Victoria, B.C., with four 3,000-ton tankers in tow, after a 4,000-mile voyage from Balboa to Victoria, September 7, 1954.

BIG, POWERFUL AND BUSINESSLIKE, Island Tug's **Island Commander,** like most of her fleet-mates, has figured in enough sea adventures to merit a book all to herself. (Photo by George N. Y. Simpson).

THE GOLIAH'S SISTER-SHIP HERCULES, towed her out from the East Coast in 1907. The **Goliah** carried extra fuel for the **Hercules.** The **Hercules** remained on San Francisco Bay, but the **Goliah** became famous on the Columbia River and Puget Sound; later returned to the East Coast.

S.S. SNOHOMISH, TOWING ISLAND YARDER with six tugs aboard, from Seattle, Washington, to Buenos Aires, Argentina, a distance of 10,000 miles—October 15, 1947 - January 14, 1948. The **Snohomish,** once a famous U. S. Coast Guard rescue tug, was purchased by the Argentine Navy after her arrival.

plants in 1933, and this heavy haul work is still an important part of the firms' activities. By 1956 the original one-tugboat operation had expanded to a fleet of 27 boats, in addition to sea-going barges, scows, salvage craft and car ferries. Many of the big barges are the sleek hulls of old sailing ships, *Star of England, Forest Friend, Betsy Ross, Sir Thomas Lipton* and other once famous sea beauties. Although they have lost their tall masts and maze of rigging, the old windjammers still give an aura of antique majesty to the 20th century working fleet of Island Tug and Barge Company.

The company engages in many activities besides log towing these days. Its salvage crews have raised vessels from seemingly hopeless positions. Company divers surveyed the hull of the Canadian Pacific liner *Princess Kathleen* after she was wrecked on the Alaska coast. The company's tug *Snohomish,* long a famous Coast Guard rescue tug in the Pacific Northwest, made towing history when she transported six 140-ton government tugboats from Seattle to Buenos Aires on one trip.

A huge barge was submerged in a floating drydock and the six tugs were guided in over it. Then, as the dock was raised, the tugs settled down to nest snugly on the broad back of the barge. The big *Snohomish* pulled the whole family of smaller boats off on their long jour-

ISLAND MAPLE, self-unloading log barge, shown loaded.

ney. She ran aground off the northeast coast of Brazil, but managed to get herself off and deliver her brood on schedule. The Argentine government was so impressed by the performance of the *Snohomish* that she was purchased for that nation's naval fleet, never returning to the Pacific Northwest. Her 20,000-mile tow remains, however, as one of the outstanding feats of the West coast tug fleet.

Company dredges have removed hundreds of thousands of yards of material from British Columbia harbors. Company divers blasted away a thousand yards of solid rock from Victoria's upper harbor. Island tugs conveyed the famous San Francisco-Sacramento stern-wheel-

er *Delta King* up the coast to Kitimat to be converted into a workers' dormitory. One of the jobs the Island tugboat men enjoyed most took place in 1945 when they helped save the great old German square-rigger *Pamir*. She was in serious trouble off Cape Flattery, in danger of drifting onto the Graveyard that claimed so many of her sisters, when the *Island Warrior* came to her assistance.

Island Tug and Barge, Ltd., has come a long way from the days of the little *Island Planet*, but the *Island Planet* is still working hard for the company. So is Harold Elworthy. He's president of one of the Northwest's biggest towing companies now.

ISLAND FIR, self-unloading log barge, demonstrating fast cargo disposal.

RESCUE SHIPS. In December, 1955, Island Tug's mighty **Sudbury** made salvage history when she brought the disabled Greek freighter **Makedonia** 3200 miles across the Pacific in the teeth of 80-mile an hour gales. Almost exactly three years earlier, in December, 1952, the **Island Sovereign** made a similar epic rescue of the Canadian Pacific freighter **Maplecove**. Detailed accounts of both sea adventures will be found in a later chapter.

TIME IS MONEY in the towing business, as in most others. Modern log barges like the **Island Logger** make loading, towing and unloading of t i m b e r products quick work compared to methods in use a few years ago.

W O R L D G L O R Y, 27,812-ton (gross) Greek oil tanker, being assisted into Esquimalt Harbour by five tugs—the two shown are **Island Comet** and **Island Trooper,** June 5, 1956.

KINGCOME NAVIGATION COMPANY

Towing of logs from a dozen logging camps, distributed over a 400-mile area from Jervis Inlet in the south to Queen Charlotte Islands in the north, is a vital operation of Canada's big Powell River Company. Equally important on the manufacturing end are the regular shipments of newsprint from the mills at Powell River to railhead and other loading centers in Vancouver. These operations involve the employment of a sizeable transportation fleet, which is under the control of Kingcome Navigation Company, a wholly-owned Powell River Company subsidiary.

This company was incorporated in 1910, with a capital stock of $10,000, for the purpose of serving the new logging operations at Kingcome Inlet, an operation that was carried on until 1925.

In 1913, capital was increased to $200,000, and the company, which now had expanded operations to the newsprint-carrying field, purchased the tugs *Ivanhoe* and *Reliance*, two

PAPER BARGES loading at Powell River Company's wharf.

paper-carrying barges and a small camp boat.

In succeeding years as plant development has expanded, the Kingcome fleet has enlarged its operations and purchased new equipment. Today there are 11 sea-going tugs flying the house flag of Kingcome Navigation. In all, Powell River Company and its wholly-owned subsidiaries operate a fleet of 33 tugs, large and small, with a combined horsepower of nearly 9,000.

The three large ocean-going tugs, *N. R. Lang* (1800 H.P.), *S. D. Brooks* (1200 H.P.), and *J. S. Foley* (1200 H.P.) are engaged almost entirely in the towing of log barges and Davis rafts from the Queen Charlotte Islands to Teakerne Arm. The rafts and barges, from 1,500,-000 feet to 2,000,000 feet, are towed singly from Cumshewa Inlet camps and Juskatla Inlet camps across Hecate Straits to a holding ground at Captains Cove on the mainland near Prince Rupert. They are later towed tandem south to Teakerne Arm. The three main species of logs produced in the Queen Charlotte camps are hemlock, spruce and cedar. The cedar, not being used in the manufacture of newsprint and pulp, is towed to Vancouver to the Powell River Company's subsidiary lumber mills.

Five other tugs, *Kingcome* (700 H.P.), *Ivanhoe* (600 H.P.), *P. B. Anderson* (400 H.P.), *Sea Lark II* (400 H.P.) and *Sea Breeze* (240 H.P.) are engaged in towing flat booms through the more protected waters between the mainland and Vancouver Island, south of the Queen Charlottes.

The tug *D. A. Evans* (350 H.P.), formerly the *Progressive*, handles all newsprint shipments from Powell River to Vancouver, towing covered barges on three regular weekly trips with an average of 700 tons of newsprint each voyage. She tows back cargoes of general merchandise such as mill supplies and equipment.

The tugs *Reliant* (265 H.P.) and *R. Bell-Irving* (240 H.P.) are used on flat booms and scows.

BIG KINGCOME NAVIGATION COMPANY TUGS like the 1200-horsepower **S. D. Brooks** (above) make quick work of hauling loaded pulpwood barges from logging camp to paper mill. Unloading from self-dumping barges like **Powell No. 2** is an even quicker operation.

PRIDE OF THE FLEET, Kingcome Navigation Company's sleek, 700-horsepower tug **Kingcome,** was built in 1952 at the Yarrow yard in Esquimalt. During much of her service this handsome ship has been commanded by Captain John "Ian" Caldwell, former skipper of the old-timer **Progressive,** built in Vancouver back in 1906.

Behind the tugs is the fleet of 13 scows and barges, seven of which are covered and designed specifically for protected shipment of newsprint. Five additional flat barges are used for carrying machinery, pulp, etc.

Another member of the fleet is the yacht *Fifer,* used to carry logging officials and executives to the widely spread camps and logging areas.

Kingcome Navigation Company is a licensed carrier. Vice-president and general manager of the company is Capt. W. Dolmage, OBE. President is George W. O'Brien.

BIG STEAM TUG LORNE was actually owned by the Puget Sound Tug Boat Company, but was registered to a Canadian corporation, the Vancouver Tug Boat Co., Ltd. This simplified customs regulations w h e n the American company had business north of the international boundary line. Here she's pictured with her 14-man crew, which was the average complement of a deep sea tug at the turn of the century.

THE J. S. FOLEY, a diesel-powered unit of the Kingcome fleet, prepares to move a deep-sea timber raft from the Queen Charlotte Islands to the booming and storage grounds at Teakerne Arm near Powell River. The rafts are towed singly from the Cumshewa camp and Juskatla Inlet camp across Hecata Strait to a holding ground at Captain's Cove on the mainland near Prince Rupert. They are later towed in tandem south to Teakerne Arm. Hemlock and spruce are used at Powell River for paper production. Cedar is towed to Vancouver for Powell River's subsidiary sawmills. (Below) The powerful **J. S. Foley** and her huge log raft are dwarfed by the timbered hills of British Columbia as they move toward the Powell River Company's booming ground at Teakerne Arm.

CAPT. JAKE IVERSON on the Vancouver waterfront, with food for his old shipmate who died and returned, so Capt. Jake insisted, in the form of a seagull. In the background, beside the totem pole, is an anchor from the fabled Hudson's Bay steamer **Beaver** of 1836.
(Photo by Andre)

AGED SEA QUEEN, Vancouver Tug Boat Company's barge **Scottish Lady**, converted to a modern rock carrier, was launched in Scotland in 1868 as the full-rigged ship **La Escocesa**, She raced such fabulous clippers as **Glory of the Seas** and **Young America**. In 1898 she came under American ownership as the **Coalinga**, later serving the Alaska Packers as the **Star of Chile**. In 1926 she was reduced to a barge and renamed **Roche Harbor Lime Transport**, but World War II saw her re-rigged as a four-masted schooner, with still another name, **Scottish Lady**, the American equivalent of her original name **La Escocesa**. She never used her fore-and-aft sails and after the war was again transferred to the British flag as the VTB barge **Scottish Lady**.

OLD JAKE AND THE SEAGULL

Captain Jake Iverson was a British Columbia tugboater of the old school. He was a character, and to the end of his days he spent part of his meagre pension to feed the ghost of a long-dead shipmate named Jack McCarthy.

Old Captain Jake wasn't more than knee-high to a capstan bar in his sea-boots, but he was as full of dynamite as the M. S. *DuPont*. He was a Norwegian, born in Christiansand and weaned on a deep-sea lead. He would give you anything he possessed and fight you at the drop of a hat.

Like a lot of seamen, Old Jake was a lover of birds and animals. In his later years, when he was a watchman for Cates Towing Company, he always had a dog and a cat, for whom he kept a budget. He always logged the weather and all other happenings. On payday he meticulously paid all his bills and put away enough money to feed his animals. The rest he blew in, in true seafaring fashion.

In addition to his dog and cat, Old Jake took good care of a waterfront seagull, whose name was Jack McCarthy. Jack and Jake had been shipmates and true friends for many a tide, but

Jack had slipped his cable, drowned, it was said, in some forgotten tragedy involving a North Pacific gale and a reef that wasn't on the chart.

Old Jake knew that the souls of true seamen take flight as gulls, so he wasn't a bit surprised when Jack came winging into Vancouver harbor and introduced himself to his old shipmate, who had swallowed the anchor and settled down as watchman at the Cates Moorings.

Every day Jake brought food for Jack, and after the gull had eaten his fill, the two old friends would sit on the edge of the pier and talk over old times. Plenty of sober Canadian waterfronters have heard those conversations between Old Jake and the seagull and they say it was a thing that gave them a sort of a creepy feeling.

Capt. Jake Iverson died last year, aged 85 or so, and Jack McCarthy flew out to sea and has not since been seen along the Vancouver waterfront.

VANCOUVER TUG BOAT COMPANY, LTD.

The Vancouver Tug Boat Company began operations in 1898 with a single 50-foot steam tug, *On Time*, operated by H. A. Jones, father of the company's present president, Harold A. Jones. By 1912 the elder Capt. Jones felt that his son was ready for an active part in the business. He gave seventeen year old Harold command of a 60-foot combination pleasure and work boat called the *Rosina K.*

Until 1917 young Jones worked the British Columbia coast with the *Rosina K.*, hunting, bartering, towing logs, freighting and engaging in any other activity that might turn an honest dollar.

On one typical voyage, Jones paused at Port Hardy to outwait a spell of gales. There he met a farmer who was bitter at the whole world because there was no market for his eggs. Young Capt. Jones offered him 25¢ a dozen for the 300 dozen he had on hand. The *Rosina K.* loaded the eggs along with her other cargo and pushed off in the teeth of a seasonal gale for Quatsino Sound.

Along the way she paused again for shelter in a convenient cove, where a lone beachcomber had built his home. Jones found the comber's house piled high with the pickings from a score of wrecked ships. He also found the sea tramp's wife much annoyed because her wandering spouse had been gone for some weeks without a word. She willingly sold everything Jones would buy in order to finance her own depar-

LA BONNE is typical of the smaller tugs of the Vancouver Tug Boat Company fleet.

ture from the lonely cove.

Back in Vancouver, the 25¢ eggs brought 40¢ a dozen and the brass from the wrecked ships brought 39¢ a pound; total profit for the voyage, above regular towing and freighting fees, $800.

With a background like that, it's no wonder that Harold A. Jones has developed Vancouver Tug Boat Company into the largest combined tug and barge fleet in British Columbia, with operations extending from Puget Sound to the Alaska Panhandle.

The elder Jones had retired from business and disposed of his tug fleet in 1919, but the lapse in the firm's operations lasted only five years. In 1924 Harold Jones incorporated the Vancouver Tug Boat Company. By the end of that year it had two boats, the 60-foot diesel *Atta Boy* and the 70-foot diesel *La Reine*.

From this start and aided by some of the industry's top executives—men like Executive Vice-President J. Arthur Lindsay and General Manager James C. F. Stewart—Jones has built the company's fleet to a total of 30 tugs ranging from 240 to 1200 horsepower. Mr. Jones completed one of the biggest B. C. waterfront deals in recent years when, in 1956, he acquired the Dolmage Towing Company, its three subsidiary companies, 16 tugs, booming and sorting grounds and other facilities, renaming it Vancouver Log Towing Company, Limited.

Vancouver Tug is especially noted for its great fleet of giant dry-cargo barges, which its powerful tugs are able to haul through northern waters, winter or summer, on railroad schedules. Like the old *Rosina K.*, the big,

modern VTB barges can haul cargoes of fresh eggs through a Queen Charlotte gale without cracking a shell.

The company's tugs, all with French names beginning with *La* or *Le,* are handled by such veteran masters as Captains Louis Perry, Bill Rumley, Art Parker, Walter Gordey, George Horton, Dave McIntosh and Gale Chute. Capt. Charles Plester, 35-year veteran of West Coast tugboating, is superintendent of the scow and barge fleet, which includes the famous old square-rigger *Scottish Lady,* ex-*Escocesa,* built at Dundee, Scotland, in 1868. Fleet maintenance is under the direction of Marine Superintendent Chris Beaton.

The company currently is building the 514-ton, 1200-horsepower tug *La Grande* for deep sea work. She will be the biggest all steel tug ever built in a British Columbia yard.

Harold Jones' company can proudly say that it plays a major role, both in boosting the economy of the province and, as a unit of the Canadian government's Air-Sea Rescue Service, in protecting its people.

COASTAL TOWING COMPANY'S steamer **Active,** built in 1889, was listed as the oldest towboat in British Columbia, but it wasn't evident when she was rebuilt and repowered with a diesel engine to become one of the West Coast's most modern towing vessels. She became a total constructive loss last year when she struck a reef, rolled over and filled on the ebb tide. (Photos courtesy Coastal Towing Co., Ltd.)

AGAINST A BACKDROP of snow-capped Canadian mountains, a Coastal Towing Company steamer eases into the company's big booming ground at Andys Bay.—(Leonard Frank Photo).

THE BIG STEAM TUG A. G. Garrish is named for the Coastal Towing Company's retired treasurer. The picture was taken in Elliott Bay when the Garrish was an entrant in a recent Seattle Maritime Day tugboat race.

MARPOLE TOWING COMPANY

Sea-going specialists are what you might call the trim boats and competent men of the Marpole Towing Company of Vancouver . . . specialists in towing barges and scows to and from a score of ports along the British Columbia Coast and Puget Sound.

The Marpole tugs do their specialized work efficiently, which is important to the shippers who entrust valuable cargoes to them and they are also popular with people who just like to *look* at tugboats. The Marpole boats, with their bright green and white hulls, varnished woodwork and shining brass, topped with diamond-marked black, red and white f u n n e l s, are among the handsomest in the Northwest.

The Marpole Company is high in the affections of steamboat fans too, for the diesel engine has not entirely dominated its fleet. Steam tugs like Captain K. Paley's handsome *Master* still bring a reminder of traditional towing methods to Puget Sound where no American-owned steam tugs remain in operation.

The company, which has offices at 1001 Main Street in Vancouver, is managed by Rufus W. Gilley, with W. A. Brown as dispatcher.

COASTAL TOWING COMPANY, LIMITED

The story of the Coastal Towing Company is the story of one man who, in the midst of a world-wide financial depression, saw one of the countless opportunities which lie in British Columbia for those with the vision and courage to sieze them. O. H. "Sparkie" New, president of Coastal Towing Company was that man.

With Capt. George P. Ellis, he formed the new company in 1937. Both men spent their savings and pledged their credit for the purchase of the new *Hyak,* a wooden diesel tug with a 120-horsepower engine. Toward the end of the year the *Hyak,* with O. H. New as skipper and engineer, put her towline on her first boom of logs. When Capt. Ellis sold out his interest in the firm Capt. Jack Ryall was hired as master of the *Hyak,* with Somerled Cameron as engineer.

It was the *Hyak,* whose picture still appears on the company letterhead, that was on hand when the M.V. *Shelco* went ashore on Stimson Reef in Johnstone Straits. She stood by and refloated the *Shelco,* afterward towing her safely to Port Neville.

The company acquired its second tug in 1939, the 52-foot *Jessie Island No. 7,* which was renamed *Hyak II* and placed in command of Capt. Aage Sonum. Capt. Sonum, who first sailed in

the Norwegian bark *Kosmos,* was skipper of the big *Active* in later years, is now port captain and vice president of the company.

Another member of the board of directors who has been with the company almost since its inception is A. G. Garrish, former secretary-treasurer, whose place in the active handling of the firm's finances has been taken by his son, H. G. Garrish. In appreciation of the years of service given to the company by the senior Mr. Garrish, the big naval steamer *Armentieres* was renamed *A. G. Garrish* when it was purchased in 1949 for conversion to a powerful freight and tow boat.

Bad luck has dogged two of the three big steam tugs purchased from the Canadian Western Lumber Comapny in 1946, the *Active, Petrel* and *Gleeful.* The *Active,* rebuilt into a beautiful and modern diesel tug, became a total loss as a result of stranding. The handsome steamer *Petrel,* a specialist at towing barges, was lost with all hands in a winter gale off Cape Mudge.

Now the company is planning new all-steel vessels of smaller size and greater power, all to be powered with Rolls-Royce diesels.

In addition to its towing fleet, the firm operates the most fully equipped booming ground on the British Columbia coast at Andys Bay on the west shore of Gambier Island . . . right in the "show-window" of Vancouver's log market. Here the big Davis and Gibson rafts can be broken down and sorted at the rate of 10,-000,000 board feet a month. A 50-ton derrick with a 108-foot boom is set over deep water where heavily laden log barges can come right alongside the beach.

The present office staff includes Port Engineer A. E. (Pat) Commins, Port Captain Sonum and Dispatcher W. D. (Bill) Mackintosh. (It's his voice you hear handing out alibis as to why the boom hasn't arrived.) Bill joined the staff as soon as he got through navigating bombers over Germany for the RCAF, and finds plotting voyages for tugboats much in his line.

President Sparkie New still keeps an active hand in the business and his watchword is "prompt delivery." The reason had better be good, company skippers have discovered, if a boom is too slow in getting to its destination. By and large, the office staff and outside crews are as smooth a working organization as the best of the diesel engines and President New seldom has cause to make a change in the line-up of Coastal Towing Company.

C. H. CATES AND SONS, LTD.

Every Northwest city of consequence has, it seems, a "Great Fire" somewhere in its history. Vancouver had one in 1886 and the town was practically wiped out. One of the first businesses to rise from the ashes was a long tent with a long table down the middle, a wood-burning cookstove in one end and a sign that said "Restaurant" outside.

The proprietor, who was a first class cook, had just removed a large roast from the oven. His partner, a first class waiter, was getting ready to serve it to the customers who were first class eaters. Just then a demolition crew touched off a charge of dynamite in the rubble outside, there was a terrific explosion and a huge stump sailed through the tent roof, demolishing both cook-stove and roast.

"This business is too damned dangerous," the restaurant's proprietor, C. H. Cates, announced. "I think I'll go back to sea." And roughly speaking that is how Vancouver's oldest tug-boat firm, C. H. Cates and Sons got its start.

Charles Henry Cates first went to sea at the age of 11, as ship's boy on the Down-East square-rigger *W. H. Weatherspoon*. After abandoning the restaurant business, he took over a remarkable vessel known as *Sprat's Ark*, an ungainly steam scow some 240 feet long with a 40-foot beam. A pair of "sewing machine" engines turned twin screws which gave the S.S. *Sprat's Ark* a speed of five miles an hour, providing wind and tide were with her.

The first log of *Sprat's Ark*, dated April, 1890, records that Capt. Cates was forced to fire his cook and chief engineer in rapid succession, not so much because they were drunk all the time as because they refused to work while in that condition. J. A. Cates, one of the skipper's brothers, was mate and he proved dependable. Convinced that they had the answer to the problem of unreliable help, C. H. and J. A. saved their money and sent for the rest of the Cates family to come out from Ragged Reef, Nova Scotia. It has been pretty much of a family business ever since. Today the business is carried on by the three sons of Capt. C. H. Cates, John, Charlie and Jim.

The first authentic Cates tug was a little steamer named *Swan*, which C. H. operated as a one-boat business. Expansion came suddenly as the result of a difference of opinion

CAPT. CHARLES HENRY CATES. The towing company he formed has become a British Columbia waterfront tradition.—(Photo from City Archives, Vancouver, B.C.)

at the old Bodega Saloon at the corner of Carroll and Cordova in Vancouver. The skipper of a rival tug, the *Stella*, announced loudly that his boat was faster than Capt. Cates' *Swan*.

"I admire your confidence," said Capt. Cates. "Let's finish our drinks and then go down and get up steam on the boats. We'll run out to Point Atkinson, hail the light keeper and come back here for another drink. The first one to finish that second drink owns both boats."

Capt. Cates proved faster than his rival and so did the *Swan*. The Cates Towing Company had doubled the size of its fleet over night. Today the firm has 14 tugs in operation, with a contract recently let for the construction of two more of the 630-horsepower "little giants" for which the Cates firm has become famous.

In 1938 Capt. Charlie was working one of the tugs when Vancouver's Pier D caught on fire and was completely destroyed. Capt. Charlie turned the tug's fire pumps on himself and his crew, sailed right into the fire and saved the lives of three trapped firemen. Skipper and crew got Royal Humane Society awards for that little job.

PLOWING UP THE WATERS of Vancouver harbor at top speed, **Charles H. Cates XI** appears to be mostly bow wave and bumper. Specially designed for harbor work by the Cates Brothers, these 630-horsepower huskies are among the most powerful boats of their size in the world.

WHEN THE BIG CARGO LINER BONANZA got tangled up with the Second Narrows Bridge, half the Cates fleet of powerful little harbor tugs was dispatched to get things under control. Performing with their usual speed and precision, they got the big ship safely away before major damage was done.

EARLY VESSELS operated by Capt. C. H. Cates included the steam scow **Sprat's Ark** (top) described by the Vancouver Daily **Province** as "one of the weirdest vessels ever to ply British Columbia waters", and the steam tug **Lois** (below). The **Sprat's Ark** was serving as flagship of the 1890 Dominion Day Yacht Races when the upper photo was taken. Downtown Vancouver of that era is in the background, with whistles of steam tugs greeting winner of the sailing race.

Capt. Charles W. Cates (right center) addressing a recent meeting of the Puget Sound Maritime Historical Society at Seattle. Steamer **Robert Dunsmuir** (right) on Cates Shipyard ways at Burrard Street and Beach Avenue, Vancouver. Capt. George Cates, owner and brother of Capt. C. H. Cates stands in left foreground, Andrew Jackson Cates, their father, in right foreground. Among other accomplishments, he supervised the construction of the first Davis raft ever made. Steamer **Robert Dunsmuir** inaugurated first regular passenger service between Vancouver and Nanaimo, later carried coal cargos from Nanaimo, earning unflattering nickname of **Dirty Bob.**—(Photo from City Archives, Vancouver, B.C.)

FAREWELL TO A FAMOUS LINER. Early in 1952 the tugs **Agnes Foss** and **Donna Foss** removed a famous old liner from the Olympia reserve fleet moorings and towed her from Puget Sound to the Panama Canal. There they were met by two Moran tugs from New York, who took the old-timer to an East Coast yard for scrapping. The liner was launched at Belfast, Ireland in 1907 as the German **President Grant.** Used as a German troop transport early in World War I, she was captured by the Allies, serving as a U. S. Army transport in both world wars. In the 20's and 30's she was in the trans-Atlantic service of the United States Lines. After service in World War II as the **Republic,** she was sold for scrap.

HEAVY STEEL CHAINS to which tug's towing lines were fastened are shown in the pictures on opposite page. Above the **Republic** is shown yawing behind the hard-working tugs. The 600-foot, 20,000-ton liner progressed in this fashion most of the way and the tug crews reported the 40-day voyage to Panama was no pleasure cruise.

Skippers of the **Agnes** and **Donna** were Ray Quinn and Mike Hilton, respectively. Below, Capt. Quinn is shown receiving the farewells of Foss executives Sid Campbell and Paul Pearson as he begins his long tow to the southward.

Left, top to bottom: Les Reynolds and Clarence Beetchum. Frank Evers in Coast Guard service. Tacoma Tugboat's **Falcon** paints a coal smoke mural on the calm skies over Puget Sound. Ed Jenner, former President of Washington Tug and Barge Company.

Right, top to bottom: Capt. Sam Wellington, Capt. Harry Butcher, recently retired as Puget Sound's senior tugboat skipper. Capt. Bert Butts of Bellingham Tug and Barge Company's **Tyee.**

COMPETITION. Sea-stained from her long voyage to Puget Sound in ballast, the big steel wind-jammer **Brabboch** is in an enviable position. With calm waters off the Cape and a mild north-westerly breeze to keep her sails drawing and offset the tricky northern current, her skipper is able to keep her under weigh for the Strait of Juan de Fuca while he haggles over towing fees with the masters of two rival tugs. Under the circumstances, the **Brabboch's** captain is likely to get a bargain rate . . . but circumstances have a way of changing fast off Cape Flattery.

DISASTER

The Pacific Northwest's first tug, *Resolute,* ended her career violently, killing most of her crew in the process. It can't be said that she thus set a precedent, for most subsequent North Coast towboats have lived out their average half-century life spans profitably and suffering only minor brushes with disaster. But there have been tragic losses among the hard-working sisterhood. The waters of America's northwest corner have their share of navigational hazards. The drifting ice and uncharted rocks and violent tide-rips of the Inside Passage to Alaska have claimed their share of towboats as well as of bigger ships.

Storms often come up violently and unpredictably, the vast ocean air masses of the Pacific constantly struggling for dominance with the Arctic cold fronts from the north. Such a sudden gale sank the tug *Velos* some 60 years ago, just as one sank the tug *Mite* in 1954. The two stories are typical of the many such tragedies that occurred in the six decades between them . . . and of others that will strike in the

years to come. The sea will never be made an entirely safe place in which to work.

The British Columbia steam tug *Velos* was helping to build the provincial parliament building at Victoria back in 1895. Towing the barge *Pilot* (the hull of the old Columbia River bar tug *Pilot*), the *Velos* was hauling building stone for the new building from the quarries on Haddington Island. There were a few whitecaps kicking up before a gusty wind when the tug swung out of Victoria harbor for a night run to the quarries on March 22, but nothing unusual. It was just a normal, boistrous March blow when the *Velos* pulled out with her barge at 9:30 p.m. Off Trial Island, outside the har-

bor, she was fighting a full southeast gale by 10 o'clock.

The wallowing barge astern made the tug unmanageable. No headway could be made, but there were men aboard the old *Pilot* and the tug skipper wouldn't cast her off. He tried to put the helm hard over, hoping to put back to the safety of the harbor, but the rudder chains broke as the little steamer began to answer her helm. It was hopeless after that. Caught broadside by a huge sea, the tug was swept helplessly in the trough to crash sickeningly against an offshore rock. She sank by the stern in a matter of seconds, only a small section of the bow remaining above water. The chief engineer, cook and one of the building contractors who was aboard, were swept overboard and drowned when the first big sea crashed aboard the wreck.

The mate managed to swing himself along the towline to the temporary safety of the barge, which was still in deep water, but the deckhand lost his grip and was swept away when he tried to follow the mate. Captain Anderson fought his way through the surf, reaching shore alive although battered half to death on the jagged rocks. The assistant engineer, clinging to the wrecked bow of the tug, died of exposure. The barge also drifted ashore on the island, but she hit the beach instead of the offshore rocks. Those aboard her, including the mate of the *Velos*, were taken off safely in the morning. But only two of the six men who had been aboard the tug lived to tell the tale of that brief, sudden storm of March 22, 1895.

The little Bellingham tugboat *Mite* was almost in her home harbor, as the *Velos* had been, when another sudden gale caught her 59 years later. The *Mite,* a tiny converted LCVP with a two-man crew, was the baby of the Bellingham Tug and Barge Company fleet. Almost diminutive enough to be rated as a "boom boat" rather than a full-fledged tug, her 165 horsepower diesel engine still made her husky enough to perform man-sized jobs. She had been up at Lummi Island pulling lost piling off the beach and rafting them for return to the booming grounds on her last assignment.

The *Mite* finished her job on January 20, 1954. She was sighted entering Hale Passage, less than 15 miles from Bellingham, that evening. As the little boat entered the pass a sudden, violent southeast storm swept in, blotting her from sight. She was never seen again.

When she failed to arrive in Bellingham there was hope, for a while, that she had put into some out-of-the-way cove for shelter or, disabled, was still afloat somewhere outside the harbor. An intensive water, shore and air search was organized that night, but hope for the little tug and her two-man crew was short lived. The bodies of skipper Robert Sloan and deckhand John Heffling were found, two days later, washed ashore on the mainland shore of the passage where their boat vanished. They wore life jackets, but had died of exposure. No trace was found of the *Mite* to give a clue as to what had happened.

Other tugboats have been battered and sunk by the big ships they were trying to help, as was the *Mogul* 60 years ago and the *Neptune* late in 1949. It's a common occupational hazard for tugboats.

The old *Mogul* had been built in 1886 at Tacoma for Captain James Griffiths and several associates, who used her, along with the tug *Collis*, to tow the old bark *Ludlow* between San Francisco and Puget Sound as a coastwise collier. The 94-foot steamer was sold to British Columbia owners in 1894, Captain Griffiths having become interested in the operation of the famous experimental "whaleback" steamship *C. W. Wetmore*. Almost completely rebuilt following her transfer, the *Mogul* had been back to work for only a short time when she was assigned to tow the British bark *Darra* from Victoria to the sea.

After letting go the hawser off Cape Flattery, the tug steamed in alongside the sailing vessel to recover the heaving line. The ship, just getting under way, swung suddenly to smash against the *Mogul's* hull. The stern was sprung by the impact; the tug was filling rapidly. Crowding on full steam, she started a race for shore but there wasn't time to get inside the strait. As she settled beneath him, the *Mogul's* skipper piled her on the ocean beach just inshore from Tatoosh Light. Her crew made it ashore, but like most ships that hit the North Pacific beaches, the stout *Mogul* was pounded to pieces by the surf before she could be rescued.

Sailing ships had vanished from the North Pacific by 1949, so it was an 8000-ton ocean steamship that did in the big steel tug *Neptune* during the November storms of that year. The diesel-powered *Neptune*, pride of the Puget Sound Tug and Barge Company fleet, had been dispatched to aid the freighter *Herald of the Morning*, disabled off the mouth of the Columbia. Fighting heavy seas in company with the San Francisco tug *Sea Fox*, the *Neptune* failed

to dodge a smashing blow from the wallowing derelict. An 8000-ton freighter packs considerably more wallop than a dainty bark and there was no time to run the *Neptune* ashore. She sank fast. There was barely time for the Coast Guard cutter *Balsam* to haul her crew to safety and second mate Martin Persson was dead before his body was pulled aboard the cutter.

Five more Northwest tugboat men fell victim of the 1949 November storms. Three died when the Vancouver tug *St. Clair* was driven ashore near Port San Juan on grim Vancouver Island, which rivals the Columbia River entrance as a marine graveyard. The big *Monarch*, fleet-mate of the *Neptune*, lost her rudder while southbound in the Inside Passage with two huge log rafts from Alaska for Everett, but her crew used an old Columbia River sternwheeler trick. Heaving the towing cable from side to side over the stern, they used the log rafts as a ponderous rudder to steer the *Monarch* to safety. Further north an Alaska Railway barge had broken loose from its tug in an earlier storm of the same month, piling ashore with a 2000-ton government cargo.

The other fatal mishap was another of the mysterious sinkings that dot the pages of North coast marine history with big black question marks. General Construction Company's *Ruby VIII* was easing an empty barge down Admiralty Inlet near Port Townsend, when one of the November storms swept in from the sea.

Later the empty barge was found anchored a few hundred feet northeast of Point Wilson Light. The tug was nowhere in sight, a mystery which was explained when it was found that the sunken *Ruby VIII* was the anchor that was holding the barge in place. The mystery of her sinking was another matter, however. Captain F. E. Gunderson and deckhand Leland Fox, the only men who had been aboard the tug, were missing. The *Ruby VIII* was raised and put back in service, but the mystery of her sinking, and of the exact fate of her crew, remained unsolved.

It was a similar story some quarter of a century earlier when the steam tug *Bahada* went missing. Along toward 2 o'clock on the morning of November 22, 1926, the *Bahada* was plodding along between Huckleberry and Saddlebag Islands, headed from Anacortes to Bellingham with a log raft. It was a quiet, routine Puget Sound night, the helmsman yawning at the big spoked wheel and most of the crew asleep in their bunks below.

The *Bahada* never made port. Something

OLD OREGON BAR TUG **FEARLESS** tried to enter the mouth of the Umpqua River one stormy night in 1889. Those on shore heard her mournful whistle-blast above the roar of the breakers, but the only sign of the **Fearless** that was ever seen again was a dead body on the beach.

happened to her in the pre-dawn darkness off Saddlebag Island, but n o b o d y is quite sure what it was to this day.

The body of crew member Bill Hansen was found the next morning on the beach at Samish Island. Near him was a lifeboat with the tug's name stencilled on the bows. Authorities wired Anacortes to report a member of the *Bahada's* crew lost overboard and drowned. There was still no suspicion that the entire vessel had been lost. But more wreckage was soon discovered on other nearby islands and the ensuing search led to the discovery of the *Bahada's* raft serenely anchored between the two islands where the tug had met her strange fate. The tow line slanted downward like a pointer to the shattered hulk of the *Bahada,* invisible under 40 fathoms of water.

The twisted and shattered condition of the wreckage led to the belief that a sudden boiler explosion had wrecked the tug and killed her entire crew. This is the generally accepted theory today, but there are some who disagree. There were reports of repeated blasts from the *Bahada's* distinctively toned steam whistle at about the time the tragedy was thought to have occurred. Shoreside residents pointed out that they recognized the *Bahada's* whistle blasts, that they could only have been distress calls, and that steam whistles don't blow on boats that have suffered sudden boiler explosions.

Powerful, unlighted rum-runners were knifing the midnight waters of Puget Sound in those days, and it was a favorite theory of many, especially n e w s p a p e r reporters, that such a speeding and piratical craft had sliced the *Bahada* in two. But, as in the case of the *Ruby VIII*, 23 years later, no one knows for sure.

It was much the same when they picked pieces of the tug *Fearless* off the beach at the mouth of the Umpqua River way back in 1889. The old *Fearless* was an 85-foot steam propeller, built at San Francisco in 1874. She went to work at Coos Bay, Oregon, the following year, remaining and growing old and somewhat creaky on the Coos Bay bar and up and down the Oregon coast between the Columbia and Umpqua Rivers.

November had been a stormy month in 1899, as it has often been before and since, but it was temporarily peaceful on the 20th, when the *Fearless* pulled away from the dock at Astoria to go wheezing across the bar and head south toward her home landing at Coos Bay. At three that afternoon the tug was sighted steaming slowly down the coast just outside the line of breakers, which were running very high as an aftermath of the most recent storm.

The short autumn day had ended by 6 o'clock when the *Fearless* reached the mouth of the Umpqua. Shore dwellers could make out the feeble g l i m m e r of her oil-burning running lights through the offshore murk and spray, and they recognized the mournful blast of her whistle. They didn't pay much attention to her, for she was a familiar coastal workhorse, she was only a few miles from home, and there was little chance that she was planning to drop into the Umpqua for a visit. The tide was ebbing and the bar was breaking, a murderous combination that would discourage a sea otter.

At 6:45 three sharp, rapid whistle blasts sounded faintly from the sea and that was the last that was seen or heard of the *Fearless* until her broken pilot house, small boat, and fragments of her hull came floating silently up the river on the incoming tide.

The body of her one passenger, a cannery operator, was found on the beach. He had crawled above the high tide line, but had died of e x p o s u r e long before help arrived. The bodies of Captain James Hill and the five crew members were never found, nor was the answer to the riddle of the steamer's complete destruction.

It was guessed that the *Fearless* had sprung a leak and filling fast, had been headed for the breaking bar of the Umpqua as a forlorn last resort. Captain Hill was too old a hand on the coast and river bars of the area to make the try under any but desperate circumstances.

Whatever tragic fate overtook her, the old *Fearless* was just one victim in a long line of

BACK IN 1909 the little 19-ton tug **Grayling** was sold by Seattle owners for work on the Panama Canal. After much difficulty, the new owners secured a six-man crew, headed by Captain A. A. Moore, had her boarded up forward and aft, and crammed with 35 tons of coal. Late in May, 1909, she passed Cape Flattery . . . and has never been seen again.

DOLLY C, of the Puget Sound Tug and Barge fleet was the victim of one of the Northwest's most recent tugboat disasters, in 1955. Although she sank in water so deep that salvage operations proved impractical, her crew was rescued by another tug.

sea mysteries that have overtaken little ships of the Northwest towing fleet t h r o u g h the years. Some areas have particularly sinister records in this regard, but few are considered more dangerous than the narrow, tideswept waters off Cape Mudge north of Vancouver, British Columbia. They have claimed many small ships and many seamen, and they seldom relinquish the bodies of their victims. The *Estelle* and the *Standard* went down there 60 years ago, and the *Petrel* in 1952; many, many small craft in the years between. The stories of all of them run much the same. Sometimes lives are saved and the story of the little ship wreck is told. More often there are no survivors, no bodies; only shattered wreckage to serve as the basis for guesses.

It was that way when the Canadian tug *Estelle* of Victoria foundered off the sinister cape six decades ago, carrying every man on board to the bottom with her. The *Estelle,* a stout 90-footer powered by a compound steam engine, left Nanaimo on February 3, 1894, to carry supplies and feed to the Vancouver Island logging camps. She was never seen again, nor were any of her eight man crew. A little wreckage drifted ashore after a while, but not enough to piece together the story of her sinking. Maybe the boiler exploded, but it was almost new

and quite sound. Probably the fierce, swirling tide-rips simply took control and sucked her down. They were as capable of doing it then as they are today.

Another Victoria tug, the *Standard,* met a similar fate a few months later—on June 17, but one man lived to tell what had happened. The *Standard* had left Victoria on June 16 with orders to coal and top off her water tanks at Nanaimo, then proceed to the Skeena River to take up her towing and freighting duties there. By half past six the next evening the little steamer was thrashing t h r o u g h heavy seas lashed up by a sudden, violent gale. As the breakers hammered her down, the great whirlpools of the Cape Mudge tide-rip reached out stealthily for her. She never had a chance, once she was in the grip of both storm and tidal millrace. She filled like a bucket in a well, sinking stern first, without a struggle.

As the steamer went under, her small boat floated off the house, riding free, but circling wildly in the tide-rip. The captain, mate and a fireman struggled to the boat, but it was a brief reprieve. The skiff overturned in a few moments, the three men thrown back into the whirlpools to be sucked from sight. The chief engineer, clinging to a flat piece of wreckage, saw his shipmates go down. Then he hung on grimly until the murderous tide-rip got tired of playing with him and tossed him into calmer water. After 12 hours afloat on his wreckage the engineer, Murray, was rescued by a trapper in a canoe.

He survived to tell the story of the *Standard's* sinking, but he appears to have lost all interest in a maritime career. An old account of the affair, published a year or so after it happened, says, "Engineer Murray is at present engaged in the powerhouse of the Victoria Street Railway Company."

It was probably a constant source of contentment to Murray to reflect that the Victoria streetcars never ran as far as Cape Mudge.

The cape hasn't mellowed any with the years. The same treacherous tides that claimed the early Canadian tugs took their latest victim two days after Christmas, 1952. The Coastal Towing Company's steam tug *Petrel* left Vancouver shortly after noon on December 27, bound for log towing duties at Gowland Harbor near Campbell River, B. C. The tug's master was told to proceed to his destination "at his convenience." Since the weather was nasty, kicking up in a manner that made log towing impossible, there was no hurry and it was suggested that he might lay over at Lund to top off his water tanks. Then the rest of the voyage could be made during daylight the next day.

It appears, however, that Captain Horrie decided to head direct for Gowland Harbor by the most direct route—through Sabine Channel and north up the Straits of Georgia. The *Petrel* was last sighted by the tug *Gleeful*, which contacted her by radio off Thormanby Island. Her normal course and speed would have placed the *Petrel* off Cape Mudge sometime between 11 p. m. and midnight. The maximum velocity of the flood tide was reached shortly before midnight that night, and the mighty flood was swirling dead against what had, by this time, become a powerful southeast wind and sweeping seas. Conditions were perfect to set the great Cape Mudge tide-rip ravening for another victim. The *Petrel* never arrived at Gowland Harbor.

About the only difference between the tragedy of the *Petrel* and those of her earlier sisters was the fact that they burned coal and she burned oil. It was a slick of fuel oil from her broken tanks that led searchers to the scene of her loss, and another Coastal Towing steamer, the *A. G. Garrish*, located the wreck lying on a ledge in 70 fathoms of water . . . at the edge of the Cape Mudge tide-rip.

The towing company's official report on the sinking concluded: "The condition of the wreckage located, the fact that no calls were received from the ship by means of radiotelephone, and that there is no evidence of any attempt being made to lower lifeboats, lead us to believe the end came very quickly and unexpectedly." It has almost always been that way, and the report added another grim bit of information:

"On making inquiries among the residents of Cape Mudge and the Campbell River district, we find that many ships have been lost in this location under similar circumstances and we feel it our duty also to say that we can find no record of the bodies of any men lost in this area having been recovered. In view of the foregoing, we conclude that this tragedy was due to the peril of the sea."

TUG BAHADA and bark **Pass of Killiekrankie.** The **Bahada** went missing.

PERILS OF THE SEA

"The peril of the sea" is a term that brings to mind great ships struggling for life in storm-swept outer reaches of the ocean. It's not a term easily associated with the commonplace little tugboats as viewed from the comfortable deck of a ferry or in the course of a waterfront stroll. Of course, when we consider the many hundreds of the little workboats in constant operation through some of the most dangerous inland and offshore waters of the continent, the percentage of wrecked boats is very small.

Some were mentioned in the last chapter . . . the *Neptune* and the *Ruby VIII* and the *St. Clair,* all lost in that one stormy November of 1949 with five men drowned. The big steam tug *Petrel,* sucked down like a toy boat in the Cape Mudge tide-rip, and five men with her. The little *Mite,* overwhelmed by a s u d d e n storm and her two-man crew washed up dead on the beach. The sudden, deadly gales of northern autumn and winter were mostly responsible for those, but the sea has other perils.

Fog is a peril of the sea; fog like the dense, dripping pall that blanketed the *Martha Foss* forging slowly up the Strait of Juan de Fuca ahead of her invisible log raft. That fog, blending with the post-midnight darkness of May 21, 1946, was typical of its breed. So thick that it felt cold and clammy to the touch and filled the nostrils with its dank smell, it congealed and dripped from deck houses and stanchions, and muffled the mournful wailing of the fog horns with its shifting, unseen mass.

The *Martha Foss* was one of the many veterans of the Northwest sea lanes still hard at work in her old age. Built at Astoria in 1886

as the 87-foot steamer *Dolphin,* she had worked the coast from the Columbia River to Puget Sound and north to Alaska for 60 years, and she was good for many years more . . . or would have been, except for that fog.

Another pioneer was groping through the dark waters off Port Angeles in that pre-dawn fog. The old steamer *Iroquois* had come around through the Straits of Magellan to run the Puget Sound passenger routes back around the turn of the century. A graceful, two-funneled express packet in those days, she was noted for her gleaming white paint and high speed. Now a Seattle-Victoria night boat for the Black Ball Ferry Line, she was ghosting through the fog, the blast of her whistle echoing eerily under the wet blanket of mist.

Up in the *Iroquois'* pilot house, her pilot had just time to reach for the whistle-pull and sound four sharp blasts when the tug's white hull showed up dimly through the fog, dead ahead. The steamer's high steel bow smashed into the w o o d - h u l l e d *Martha Foss* almost square amidships and she heeled far over, mortally stricken. Fortunately the *Iroquois* was not moving fast enough to swamp the tug under her bows, and she stayed afloat for a few minutes; long enough for the crew of the *Iroquois* to take off the men of the *Martha Foss.* All of them, that is, except second engineer Nelson Gillette. On watch below, he was crushed to death in the wreckage of the tug's hull as the Black Ball liner's bow struck.

Six of the *Martha Foss'* seven-man crew lived to sweat out other Puget Sound fogs, but it doesn't always work out that way. When the

war surplus tug *W. H. McFadden* went down in the Strait of Juan de Fuca a year after the *Martha Foss*, there were no survivors at all to tell what peril of the sea had struck the *McFadden*.

The *McFadden* was not a beautiful craft. Originally built for the government as a Mississippi River tug, she looked top-heavy and it was no optical illusion. Her high-piled deck houses were made of three-eighths inch steel. Even her big dummy stack was hollowed from thick steel. The fortunes of war somehow found her at Seattle when hostilities ended, and she was known along the waterfront there as the "Beer Barrel" . . . a tribute to her strange design.

Following a period of layup at Kennydale, the *McFadden* was purchased by a Texas firm and a crew signed on to take her around to New Orleans by way of San Pedro and Panama. Somebody had a lot of misplaced confidence in the 68-foot tug's sea-going qualities, apparently, for she foundered on the first night of her voyage before she even reached the open sea.

First news of the disaster came when the Richfield Oil tanker *Topila* reported having sighted a dead man floating in a life jacket off Dungeness Spit. The Coast Guard, investigating the report, picked up three more floating bodies, spotted an oil slick and wreckage in the waters off Dungeness. It was apparent that some grim fate had caught up with the *McFadden* and her crew.

THE WANDERER WANDERS ON TO A SANDBAR. One of Puget Sound's most famous tugs, the **Wanderer** is the subject of many fine yarns. C. Arthur Foss tells this one: "Some years ago the captain of the **Wanderer,** upon arriving at Tacoma after a stormy voyage, reported to Henry Foss. Henry fixed his bilious eye on Captain Cameron and asked the condition of the tug.

Cameron reported, "Sir, the **Wanderer** is leaking."

"Leaking," said Henry. "Leaking, that's all I hear. The **Wanderer** is leaking! The **Wanderer** is leaking! If it is not presuming too much on your intelligence, Captain Cameron, just where is the **Wanderer** leaking?"

With a guileless look on his face Cameron replied, "Henry, where does a basket leak?"

Needless to say, the **Wanderer** was sent to dry dock immediately."

There was a good deal of conjecture as to just what had happened. Jefferson County authorities surmised that an explosion might have wrecked the tug, for the bodies that were found were badly crushed and bruised. Coast Guard investigators were of the opinion that the topheavy little craft had been caught in a tide-rip and cross sea that capsized her, throwing four of the crew into the water, trapping the other four inside as she went down. Waterfront opinion agreed with the Coast Guard theory. The *McFadden* was undeniably topheavy and her fuel tanks carried no baffles to prevent her heavy load of fuel from flowing back and forth as she rolled. In a heavy sea and rip tide these design faults could easily combine to result in sudden tragedy. But it's

THE DEEP-SEA TUG NEPTUNE sank off the Columbia River bar after a collision with the steamship **Herald of the Morning.** A new **Neptune,** launched at Portland in 1956, has replaced the lost vessel in the Puget Sound Tug and Barge fleet.

mostly guesswork when a ship goes down in deep water and nobody lives to tell what happened.

Every year the peril of the sea is faced by the North Coast tugboats, and every year a few of them meet temporary or permanent defeat. In 1951 the Canadian *Nor'west* burned and the *Ironbark* stranded in British Columbia waters. The *Marlyn* foundered in a summer blow in the harbor at Nehalem, Oregon, and a man of her crew was drowned. Up on the Alaska route the big Miki type towboat *Macloufay* collided with the smaller 97-foot *Andrew Foss,* sending her to the bottom with the loss of one life.

After that the *Petrel* foundered, killing all her crew. Up in Rosario Strait the *Baer* sank after striking a shoal. The big Pacific salvage steamer *Salvage King* was gutted by fire and sank in Victoria harbor. The little *Mite* went down with her crew. Considering the miles covered and the hazards faced, the list is small, but the dangers are there and sometimes your luck runs out. When it does a tugboat can sink as deep as the *Titanic* . . . and much faster.

The big Vancouver tug *C. P. Yorke* went down so fast that only two of her crew escaped . . . and they by a miracle . . . when she slammed into an unnamed reef on December 11, 1953.

The *Yorke,* owned by the Car Barge Towing Company, was rolling and pitching through high seas and dense, wind-driven rain 40 miles northwest of her home port when she met disaster. The heavy barge she was towing astern was hardly visible, except for the glimmer of white water as the seas crashed against the blunt bow. It was nasty weather and tricky waters and there was no visibility to speak of.

Off Buccaneer Bay the *Yorke* swept down on the hidden rock reef. The sudden shock and rending of the death blow; the icy water flooding in a cataract through the smashed hull and then, in a matter of minutes, the tug is awash from stem to stern. Skipper Roy Johnson was able to get off one brief S. O. S. message before he was swept from the sinking tug into the numbing water. Looking back, he saw the blind, clumsy bows of the barge loom out of the rain, still following in the track of the wrecked tug. He saw the ponderous barge crash into the wreck, to which men were still clinging, completing the work of destruction.

A fishing boat, answering the tug's single radio distress call, picked up Captain Johnson, alive but unconscious and two-thirds frozen, from the water. Later, chief engineer Bill Mac-Donald was found lying on a beach 12 miles from the scene of the wreck. Somehow he had managed to cling to a smashed, overturned lifeboat during 12 freezing hours. Finally, too numb with cold to keep his grip any longer, he gave up the long fight for life. He was washed ashore after he had given up hope.

The two survivors were hospitalized at Pender Harbor, recovering in time to attend the funeral services for three of their less fortunate shipmates, whose bodies were recovered in widely separated areas miles from the wreck. Two other bodies were not recovered.

Divers found the shattered *Yorke* lying on a pinnacle rock only 40 feet below the surface, but teetering dangerously on the edge of a 500-foot dropoff. As divers struggled to work slings around the hull, the powerful currents swept against the wreck, constantly threatening to push it into deep water beyond recovery. Several times she lurched from her precarious ledge, scraping even closer to the edge as the divers scrambled for safety. At last, however,

the slings were rigged and two powerful derrick barges, working with the big tug *Salvage Queen,* hoisted what was left of the *Yorke* to the surface.

The roll of lost tugs is a long and continuing one. The 148-foot Vancouver tug *Chelan* lost with all hands off the Alaska Panhandle in April, 1954; the 66-foot *Dolly C.* sunk by her barge off Whidbey Island in August, 1955—her 5-man crew rescued by the *Titan.* There are big dangers facing the men who go down to the sea in little ships.

Such perils of the sea as sudden storms and hidden reefs are not confined entirely to the salt water of ocean, sound and straits. The river towboats have hazards of their own and they sometimes get into trouble. It was a combination of storm and underwater obstacle that almost finished off Portland's pet steamboat, the old stern-wheeler *Henderson,* a few years back. Fortunately the *Henderson* is a grand old lady with a fighting heart, and she's blessed with a crew who were willing to stay with her when the going got tough. So she survived her dangerous ordeal to the unconcealed delight of her thousands of loyal fans, who are aware that the Columbia River wouldn't be the same without the *Henderson.*

The trouble started along about five o'clock of a dark, cold and generally unpleasant De-

THE HERCULES, shown here passing a Canadian Pacific "Princess" liner, has had her share of narrow escapes from the Peril of the Sea.

cember morning in 1950. Off Longview, Washington, a driving rain dimmed the river lights while big whitecaps hissed to the push of an icy wind. Out in the river the dark bulk of the 7600-ton decommissioned freighter *Pierre Victory* loomed through the rain and driven spray. Her powerful diesels throbbing, the Shaver Transportation Company's steel towboat *Chinook* kept the forward hawser taut as she guided the unpowered steamship into the bend of the channel on the Washington side of Cottonwood Island. It was a struggle. The shrieking wind and nasty cross-chop made the high-riding freighter almost unmanageable. Back aft, the stern-wheel steamer *Henderson* puffed and splashed along at the *Pierre Victory's* starboard flank, her blunt bows shoving hard against the towering ship's stern, her big paddle wheel and multiple rudders biting deep in the wind whipped river.

The freighter and her two escorting towboats had left Portland at midnight, bound for the reserve fleet anchorage near Astoria, where the victory ship was scheduled for mothball storage. The wind and rain had been building

up all night. Now, just before dawn, it was reaching its full fury. As gusts shoved hard against the freighter's port side, the *Chinook's* diesels rumbled at full power against the tautly angled hawser; the *Henderson*, her steam engines coughing gently, shoved hard against the lee side.

In spite of their efforts, it was evident to the river pilot, high on the freighter's bridge, that dangerous leeway was being made. The low, wooded bulk of Cottonwood Island was coming out of the murky darkness to meet them. The inter-ship telephone in the *Henderson's* pilot house jangled, and in answer to the call from the big ship, bells jangled in the stern-wheeler's engine room. As the beat of the paddle-buckets quickened, Pilot Don Weik swung the big, spoked steering wheel to left rudder. Slowly the stubborn hulk of the freighter payed off to the left, heading up into the proper channel again.

Then real trouble began. A tremendous blast of wind slugged against the struggling ships, pressing the *Henderson* far over until the seas were breaking clear across her low main deck. Galley gear and loose fittings crashed as the old paddler careened wildly, and the towing lines to the freighter drew bar-tight, vibrating under the strain until the shouted orders of the pilot brought a gang to slack them off. The inexorable current and howling wind were pressing the ships ever closer to the dark bulk of the island to starboard.

The gallant old paddler recovered herself and with every ounce of steam at work, rudders swung to full left, she shouldered the helpless freighter back toward the open river again.

Then, with a sickening crash, the *Henderson* lurched to a momentary halt. The jagged pilings of a forgotten island dock, well hidden below the swirling surface of the river, had reached out to impale the struggling steamboat. She hung, stricken and motionless, for only a moment. Then the towing lines drew taut again, the moving bulk of the freighter dragging the towboat helplessly across the width of the sunken dock, each watersoaked snag in turn ripping deep into the wounded hull.

In minutes the main deck was awash, off-watch crewmen battering their way out of the sprung compartment doors in the steeply listing superstructure. As water poured into the engine room the boiler fires were secured. Things couldn't have looked much darker for the last of the old time Columbia River stern-

THE MAGIC, a 67-foot steam tug, built at Port Blakely in 1893, crowded the war news off the front pages of Seattle papers briefly in 1917 when she sank a passenger steamer in Elliott Bay. The Sound steamer Tolo, outward bound from Seattle for Bainbridge Island, was run down by the Magic in a pea-soup fog.

The Tolo, with 53 passengers aboard, sank in less than eight minutes, but the Magic's whistle blasts brought other steamers to the scene and most of the wreck victims were rescued. Two women passengers and the Tolo's Chinese cook were drowned. One man died of exposure after reaching Bremerton on the rescue steamer H. B. Kennedy.

The Tolo, originally the Camano, had been sunk in an earlier disaster, having been rammed by the Sound steamer Sioux in Everett harbor. The Magic did a more thorough job of it and the little passenger steamer was not salvaged.

wheelers. Captain Sidney Harris had just two choices. He could abandon ship, taking to the small boats and leaving the old paddler to founder in mid-river, or he could try to beach her.

The lines to the freighter were cast off, leaving the *Chinook* alone at the end of the bow hawser. Lurching free, lines trailing alongside, waves smashing over her hull, the *Henderson*

The **Ruby VIII** was less fortunate. She sank with the loss of all hands.

struggled down stream, reeling and fighting her way slowly, like a wounded animal.

As she clawed her way closer to the foot of the island and the safety of the shoals, she sank lower and lower in the water, listed further over to the weight of water in her torn hull, but the deserted engines hissed on above the rising water and the stern-wheel still turned. It took seven minutes to reach the foot of the island and round it, and every second of it was touch and go. But somehow the game old lady and her fighting crew made it. Slipping easily up on the smooth sand bottom, she settled down with a tired sigh in less than nine feet of sheltered, safe water. Back aft, the big wheel still turned, slowly and futilely, on the last of the expiring steam, but it was no longer needed. The grand old lady of the river was safe!

But out in the river the *Chinook* was fighting for her life with the wildly careening bulk of the *Pierre Victory*. Rampaging down stream against the full thrust of her roaring diesels and foaming screw, the tug fought back against the almost irresistible pull of river, storm and ship. It was many minutes before the full power of the tug's engines began to make themselves felt. But at last the shore lights slowed their swift movement astern. Slowed and grew stationary, as the *Chinook* brought the huge ship up on her hawser like a roped bull that has finally given up the fight.

FAVORITE SHORESIDE HANG-OUT for tugboat men on the Seattle waterfront was the old Pier 3 Cafe. Here proprietors George Jasper and Del Gaffne serve suds to a salty crew of waterfronters.

Then the *Chinook* held the victory ship in mid-channel until other tugs, summoned by radio, arrived to take over for the battered *Henderson*. With their help the troublesome freighter was hauled off to join the mothball fleet without further incident.

As for the old stern-wheeler, she was raised and towed back to Portland, where the 20-foot gash in her hull was patched up and she was back at work again in a few weeks. Portlanders, hearing her mellow whistle sounding for the bridges, felt that they owed something to Captain Harris and the rest of the *Henderson's* crew. They saved more than just an old stern-

wheeler that perilous early morning on the river. They saved a river institution.

The stern-wheel steamer *Henderson* was a leading lady of the movies recently, when she played the part of a 19th century river boat in the technicolor production "Bend in the River." But none of her celluloid adventures were as spine-chilling as her real life brush with disaster that December morning off Cottonwood Island. Her crew risked their lives to save her, and when neither crew nor ship will give up fighting they can often overcome "the peril of the sea."

Cook Whitey Bergren shows Joe Williamson what happens to marine photographers who come back to the galley once too often.

Crews of harbor tugs can usually get to a barber shop at regular intervals, but the men of the deep-sea boats sometimes have to settle for this.

Wheel watch. Capt. Chet Thurness at the helm.

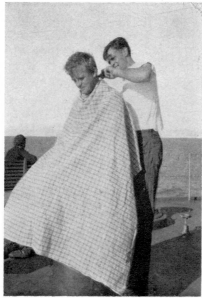

GOLIAH

In many ways, Puget Sound's second *Goliah* was typical of the Northwest's big deep water steam tugs, both in appearance and in the work she did. Built in 1907 by John Dialogue of Camden, New Jersey, the *Goliah* and her sister tug, *Hercules,* were massive, powerful steel steamers, 151 feet long, 27.1 beam and 15.2 depth, with a speed of better than 13 knots.

The two boats came to the West Coast, via Cape Horn, the *Hercules* towing the *Goliah,* which was loaded with extra fuel for the *Hercules'* boilers. In San Francisco they went to work for the Shipowners' and Merchants Tugboat Company, but in 1909 the Puget Sound Tug Boat Company sent Capt. Buck Bailey and port engineer J. F. Primrose to the Bay City to have a look at the *Goliah.* Their report was enthusiastic and the Puget Sound Company bought her. Capt. T. H. Cann piloted her north from San Francisco.

Shortly after World War I the *Goliah* returned to the East Coast, having been sold as the sailing ship trade of the Puget Sound Tug Boat Company diminished. During the years she operated in the Northwest she had the comfortable reputation of a "lucky ship." This in spite of the many hazardous exploits in which she engaged.

In 1916, skippered by Capt. T. Nielsen, the *Goliah* snatched the disabled N o r w e g i a n freighter Niels Nielsen from almost certain destruction on the lee shore of Vancouver Island, a feat which has been vividly described by R. H. (Skipper) Calkins, Associate Editor of the

Marine Digest, in his book *High Tide,* published in 1952.

One of the *Goliah's* specialties was the towing of big Cape Horn windjammers up the coast when they had a deadline charter to meet on Puget Sound. In January of 1914 the *Goliah* set a new speed record for herself by towing the big American square-rigged ship *Aryan* from the Golden Gate to Victoria in 88 hours and 30 minutes. The *Aryan,* last wooden square-rigger built in America, was a heavy-hulled cargo carrier due to load nearly two million feet of timber for South Africa, and tugboat men agreed that her fast trip north was quite an accomplishment, even for the *Goliah.*

In June of the same year the *Goliah* set a new Alaska towing record, beating the one she had set two years earlier. Towing the barge *James Drummond* northbound and the barge *St. James* southbound, she completed the round trip between Seattle and Gypsum, Alaska— 1900 miles—in 10 days and 12 hours. Both barges were loaded to capacity, but in their younger days they had been noted clipper ships, their fine-lined hulls helping the powerful *Goliah* to set another towing record.

Of course, even the mighty *Goliah,* a craft still looked upon by many veteran Northwest tugboat men as the finest ever to ply those waters, had her spells of bad luck. Back in the late winter of 1909 she was engaged in towing the barge *Quatsino* loaded with ore from southeastern Alaska to Seattle. With pilot T. H. Cann

THE SECOND GOLIAH RESCUED MANY SHIPS, both sail and steam. Here she's shown bringing the disabled freighter **Washington** in from the Pacific.

at the wheel, the *Goliah* was nosing her way through a pea-soup fog off the British Columbia coast, the pilot hoping to pick up the dim glow of the government light which was normally kept burning at the north tip of the island. Unfortunately, the Green Island light was out that night, and when Cann did pick up the fog-shrouded glimmer of a beacon it was actually a surveyor's marker on neighboring Gray Island.

Cann steered for the light, planning to take the *Goliah* and her tow through the narrow channel just off Green Island which was a favorite shortcut of tugboaters along this route. He didn't realize until too late that he was heading for Gray Island, where there was no channel. The *Goliah* took a shortcut all right,

but it was an overland route, and she didn't get very far, ending up high and dry on the beach with the heavily laden barge beside her. The tug was floated without damage, but the barge *Quatsino* and the cargo of ore were total losses.

Almost exactly a year later the *Goliah* ran into more bad luck while engaged in towing a big barge, this time with more tragic results. At that time the tug was hauling rock from Waldron Island, in the San Juans, to Grays Harbor, where it was used in the construction of the jetties at Westport. A fleet of nine seagoing barges was used to transport the rock, all of them stripped-down sailing ships like the *Palmyra, Big Bonanza, Corondolet, James Drummond* and *St. James,* all of them staunch

THE SCHOONER GARMS was in even worse plight than this, but the **Goliah** towed her to safety after a nick-of-time rescue from the "Graveyard" of Vancouver Island.

and seaworthy, and all but one of well over a thousand tons register. The smallest of the fleet was the ex-schooner *Wallacut,* built at Portland, Oregon, in 1898 and rated at 708 gross tons. This was the barge the *Goliah* was towing from Puget Sound to Grays Harbor in October of 1910. The story of what happened is contained in a shipping bulletin datelined Port Townsend, October 5, 1910:

"*The loss at sea of Andrew Henderson, aged 24, and Hans Christensen, aged 25, from the rock barge* Wallacut *is the latest of the long list of casualties due to the gale in the North Pacific Sunday. The men were swept from the barge while it was in tow of the tug* Goliah *at six o'clock in the morning off Destruction Island, while the craft, deep-laden with stone for Grays Harbor jetty work, was contending against a sea so furious it seemed almost certain to cost the lives of the five men constituting the barge's crew.*

"*A report of the tragedy was brought here by Captain John Jarman, master of the barge, whose command was forced to return to Neah Bay after vainly trying for 30 hours to cross the bar into Grays Harbor.*

"*Captain Jarman attributes the loss of his men to the unsafe action of Captain Bailey of the* Goliah, *in putting to sea against most hazardous storm conditions. He states that when the tug and barge passed out at Cape Flattery Saturday night, the sea was so high that he used every endeavor to warn the tug not to attempt the run down the coast.*

"*When well outside the waves rose so high and the wind grew so violent that Captain Jarman states he would have taken his crew and attempted to make shore at any time after getting past Flattery had the barge possessed anything in the way of adequate lifeboats.*

"*A point near Grays Harbor bar was eventually reached, the barge leaking badly, and under weather conditions that prevented making an effort to pass into Aberdeen. With this*

THE POWERFUL GOLIAH was a classic example of the finest type of deep-water steam tug.

plan frustrated, the tug turned for a return course to the Sound. While Henderson was about to relieve Christensen at the wheel, a wave more furious than any of the others that had threatened to send the barge to the bottom, broke in a big curling comber over the weather rail, sending both men clear of the ship and into the sea. The accident was witnessed by Captain Jarman and his two other sailors, but no aid could be given.

"Captain Jarman is a veteran on the North Pacific and describes the storm through which he passed as the most severe experienced in these waters."

Captain Buck Bailey, who was skipper of the *Goliah* that trip, was noted for laughing in the teeth of the North Pacific when it was in its worst moods, frequently taking whatever big Puget Sound Tug Boat Company craft he was piloting into dangers which kept all other deep-sea towboats safe at anchor. If he miscalculated that time, at the cost of two lives, he made it up many times over in daring rescue operations which made him famous the whole length of the Pacific Coast.

At the termination of the rock-towing contract, the *Goliah* steamed down the coast to take her station off the Columbia River mouth. The Puget Sound Company had decided to set up a pilotage and towing service there in opposition to the established bar tugs. The *Goliah*,

with ample accommodations and oil tanks capable of stowing a month's supply of fuel, was well designed for such service, and she spent most of her time cruising off the lightship day and night, with her bar pilots aboard.

It was after the termination of her piloting duties off the Columbia that the *Goliah* performed a rescue exploit which was even more dramatic than her later saving of the *Niels Nielsen*. Unfortunately, there was no newspaper man aboard that time, so the adventure has never been fully told.

The story began, for the *Goliah*, on January 9, 1914, when the schooner *Crescent*, which had sailed from Everett for Newcastle on December 22, came limping back to Clallam Bay with a part of her deckload gone and her cabin stove in. Her captain, thankful to have gotten back inside Cape Flattery with his ship still afloat, reported having seen another schooner, the *William F. Garms*, dismasted, leaking, and in sore distress 100 miles southwest of the Cape. The *Garms*, a four-masted schooner of 1,094 tons gross register owned by Olson and Mahone of San Francisco, had sailed from Coupeville on December 28 with a full cargo of mining timbers for Sanata Rosalia, Mexico. She was commanded by Captain F. Turloff and carried a crew of ten men.

As soon as word of her peril was received, the Puget Sound tugs *Goliah*, *Tyee* and *Lorne* headed out from Port Townsend to search for her. With them went the lifesaving tug *Snohomish* from the Port Angeles Coast Guard base, while the big Port of Portland tug *Oneonta* went smashing across the Columbia bar to join in the search.

With a full hurricane lashing the sea to maniac fury, the tugs were hard put to keep afloat, and the search became one long, wet nightmare, in which only the hardiest and most seaworthy could survive. The *Oneonta*, veteran of many a hairbreadth rescue off the Columbia, was never able to get more than 15 miles to sea. Even the *Snohomish*, especially designed as a rescue cutter for North Pacific waters, took such a beating that she was barely able to keep at sea. The mighty *Goliah* surged into the lead of the rescue fleet and she stayed there until the end, handling things almost single handed.

After leaving Coupeville with her holds full and her deck piled high with timber, the *Garms* had failed to pass Cape Flattery on her first try. Finding wind and sea too much to face, Captain Turloff had put her about to anchor overnight in Clallam Bay, the first sheltered anchorage inside the Cape. The following day the deeply laden schooner tried again, and this time she made it. New Year's Day of 1914 found her laboring in gray, ominous seas a hundred miles offshore and a little north of the Columbia River entrance. The wind was not unduly high, but the big Pacific rollers were still writhing and hissing from the harrassment of previous storms.

Captain Turloff was taking no chances with the caprices of North Pacific winter. When, near midnight, several blasts of gusty wind struck the ship to give emphasis to the warning of the fast falling barometer, he ordered all sails reefed down. At dawn the next morning it was blowing hard and the glass was down to 28.50. Before noon the storm had become a near-hurricane. The schooner was able to stand up to the steady pressure of the wind, but this was no ordinary storm. Great, shrieking hurricane gusts came tearing across the ocean at intervals to hammer the ship like monstrous fists, making the normal background of the storm seem peaceful by comparison.

One such blast, whistling through the schooner's bare poles, tore the mizzen mast out by the roots and flung it overside. With the situation now becoming desperate, the captain tried to wear ship. Mate Chris Hansen, a grizzled veteran of more than half a century at sea, led

the crew in setting the peak of the double reefed foresail and half the square sail on the foremast, but the storm had taken full control and it did no good. The schooner would not answer her helm.

Another mighty gust sledgehammered the staggering ship, smashing her over on her side until the remaining masts were in the water. The captain ordered the crew to cut the lashings which held the deckload, hoping that the ship would right herself when relieved of this topheavy weight. The men clawed their way over the deck, which was now as perpendicular as a wall, loosening turnbuckles and freeing cables. The sweeping seas helped with this work, and at intervals for three hours the thunder of the great timbers hurtling over the side could be heard above the roar of the hurricane and the shrieking of the tortured rigging.

The timbers took the main and jigger masts with them, leaving only the stump of the foremast standing above the ruined deck, but the ship had been saved, temporarily at any rate. Relieved of the weight of masts and deckload, she slowly rolled back almost to an even keel. The three broken masts, splintered and dangerous as battering rams, were still fast to the rolling, pitching derelict, tangled in the rigging of the still-standing foremast. Just when it seemed that the *Garms* could no longer withstand the added punishment of the careening masts, she rolled in the trough of the sea, fell over on her side, and, with a splintering crash, the last remaining mast fell. The schooner shook herself free as the tangled mass of spars and rigging went by the board, tearing out the heavy bowsprit and taking it with them.

It was then 4:30 in the afternoon. Five hours before, the *Garms* had been a staunch ship without a scar on her. Now she was a floating hulk without a mast standing and with opened seams taking in water fast.

In this condition she rode out storm after storm until, on January 7 the schooner *Crescent* was sighted, badly battered and leaking, but with her masts still standing. When the *Crescent* clawed in past Flattery two days later to report the *Garms'* desperate situation the long and dangerous search for her began.

The storms did not abate as the three big commercial tugs and the *Snohomish* put to sea on their rescue mission. The whole coast, from California to Alaska was being hammered mercilessly. The weather bureau station at North Head reported wind velocities of from 84 to 92 miles an hour. Seas smashed out the thick glass lantern at the Trinidad Head lighthouse, near Eureka, putting out the light which normally towered 200 feet above the reach of the sea. On the night of January 3, the Columbia River and Umatilla Reef lightships were torn from their two-ton moorings off the coast and sent staggering for safety, leaving only the Swiftsure lightship in place, rolling on her beam ends, steaming at full power against the hurricane to relieve the strain on her moorings.

In the midst of this watery chaos, the *Garms* was drifting northward helplessly toward the Vancouver Island Graveyard. Her rudder and steering gear had been carried away by later storms, leaving her totally at the mercy of the elements. After two weeks of merciless punishment, no sleep and little food, the schooner's crew sighted the light on Triangle Island at the northern tip of Vancouver Island. Under orders from the captain, they got a small boat overside, but it immediately filled and sank. They tried again with one of the two remaining boats but it too was capsized and lost in the terrible seas which were sweeping them toward certain destruction on the outlying reefs of north Vancouver Island.

When the *Garms* had drifted to within 600 yards of the spouting reefs, the captain, as a last resort, ordered the anchors dropped. Surprisingly, they held.

With no help in sight, and with his ship, or what was left of it, rolling helplessly in the very backwash of the deadly reefs, Captain Turloff called for volunteers to man the one remaining lifeboat. Five men responded and, with the captain at the steering oar, the boat left the ship to fight its way toward more inhabited parts of Vancouver Island where help might be summoned.

Soon after the boat left, the five remaining members of the *Garm's* crew under Mate Hansen were horrified to see another black storm sweeping in from the southwest. Soon the *Garms* was straining at her anchors like a mad stallion, and every man aboard knew that she could not hold for long. With the last small boat gone there was no hope for them unless rescue came soon, and as yet there was no sign of a rescue ship.

When, shortly after noon on January 14, Captain Thomas Nielsen brought the *Goliah* rolling and pitching up from the south and caught his first glimpse of the *Garms* he shook his head sadly and called for the tug's radio operator. A few hours later the extras were on the streets in Seattle with a story of disaster.

"SCHOONER GARMS FOUND ON ROCKS!

"Wireless message from Capt. T. Neilsen of tug Goliah *says schooner is piled up on Haycock Island.*

"Unable to see if men are clinging to vessel.

"The schooner William F. Garms *is a wreck on West Haycock Island 15 miles west of Cape Scott, the northernmost point of Vancouver Island. The fate of Captain F. Turloff and the crew of 10 men will be known within a few hours.*

"News of the fate of the schooner which, for more than a week, has been drifting helplessly and waterlogged a derelict outside Cape Flattery, was received in two wireless messages from Captain T. Neilsen, master of the Puget Sound Towboat Company's tug Goliah. *The first came shortly after noon and this was supplemented later by a brief dispatch giving the exact location of the vessel."*

Captain Neilsen had just been able to make out the *Garms* on the rocky shore of the island when he sent the message and said that he expected to be alongside the ill-fated craft by one o'clock.

Fortunately, however, Captain Neilsen's first impression had been wrong. Certainly the

RESCUE. The disabled Norwegian freighter **Niels Nielsen,** with the twin disks in her rigging signaling "not under control" was perilously close to the lee shore of Vancouver Island when the tug **Goliah** came to the rescue. This picture was taken as the **Goliah's** mate flung a heaving line toward the freighter. One of the **Nielsen's** crew stands ready to secure the line, while at the winch other Norse seamen prepare to bend on a towing cable. The **Niels Nielsen** rescue took place in November, 1916.

GOLIAH TOWING BARGE WALLACUT. On one such voyage two crew members were swept from the **Wallacut's** deck and drowned in heavy seas off Grays Harbor.

Garms looked a total wreck, lying dismasted in the spray of the seas breaking on the Graveyard rocks, but she was not quite finished yet. When the *Goliah* worked in closer it was seen that the wrecked schooner was still afloat a few yards outside the reefs, but that her safety and the lives of her crew were almost literally hanging by a thread.

Ironically, it was when they saw salvation surging alongside them in the form of the deep-sea tug *Goliah* that the *Garms'* crew came closest to final disaster. The relief was too much for them. After their seemingly unending struggle against death they went to pieces completely when they saw the *Goliah* coming. All five of them, from grizzled old Hansen to the Japanese cook stood on the careening deck laughing and crying like hysterical children. When the line which was to tow them from certain death to safety was fired from the *Goliah's* deck, the stupified sufferers on the schooner didn't seem to know what it was or what to do with it. They could only cackle and smile and wave trustingly at the *Goliah's* men.

It was pathetic, and it was terribly frustrating to the tugboat men. The barometer had been low before, but now the bottom seemed to be dropping out of the glass. It was obvious that a storm was coming that would dwarf the previous hurricanes.

Finally Mate Hansen's sea-training gained control over his own shattered nerves and that of his men. The towline was made fast, but it had taken six hours, instead of a few minutes, as it should have. Winter night had already blotted out sea and shore, bringing with it the first great gusts of the oncoming storm. Time was fast running out.

There was no time to get the schooner's anchors in. Hansen led the crew forward, unshackled the chains and let the anchors go. The *Goliah* belched a great cloud of black smoke as she swung around with the foam boiling under her broad counter. With all her 1500 horsepower at work she dragged the hulk of the schooner away from the reaching fingers of the Graveyard. It wasn't a moment too soon. By the time the tug and her wallowing tow had reach the lee of Vancouver Island the hurricane was raging at a hundred miles an hour. If the *Goliah* had been a single hour later, the *Garms* and her crew would have been smashed to pulp on the offshore reefs.

At about the time the *Goliah* reached the relative safety of the strait with the *Garms* in tow, the cutter *Snohomish* had picked up a half-sunken lifeboat in the sweeping eye of her searchlight. The big rescue tug had been swept and gutted by the storm as she cruised almost a thousand miles in the teeth of seas that had flooded the ship, torn out the quarter davits, and carried away much of the deck gear, but her crew was still alert and ready for business. The nearly swamped boat was taken aboard with the entire remaining crew of the *Garms* alive but completely exhausted. Captain Turloff had to be carried to the cutter's wardroom.

An hour later the wind had reached its full velocity and the seas were so huge that no lifeboat could possibly have survived in them.

SALVAGE CHIEF

(This story first appeared in the magazine, Ships and the Sea, Kalmbach Publishing Co., Milwaukee, Wis., under the title, "Seagoing Specialist")

December 8, 1952. For days the bitter storms of Northwest winter had been sweeping in to send the white surf thundering on the flat sand beaches of the Washington coast. From the mouth of the Columbia to Juan de Fuca entrance the gray coast looked the same; dark, wind-tossed forests inland above the miles of hard packed ocean sand. And offshore the great Pacific rollers met the inhospitable coast in a great welter of roaring, smoking surf. A mile offshore the surf was breaking, and the tossing line of white extended north and south with hardly a break for a hundred and fifty miles.

Willapa Harbor entrance, north of the Columbia, was hidden in the wet fury of wind driven rain and breaking surf. Still further north, the Grays Harbor bar was another storm-lashed question mark in the long scroll of fury the southwest gales were writing on the Washington coast.

The long stone fingers of the Grays Harbor jetties were almost invisible under the tons of cold gray water that smashed against them to leap high in the air like thwarted monsters. The great rocks shifted and groaned under the battering impact of the sea. Inshore the storm warning flags streamed, shredding in the wind's blast above the Coast Guard lookout station. Below them the station's air horn blasted out at its fixed interval. The low moaning of the whistling buoy on the bar was unheard in the wind and rain and smashing seas, as ineffectual as the wildly rolling bell buoys further down the bay.

It seemed unlikely that any ship would need their guidance that day, in any event. At Westhaven the fishing fleet lay huddled together like so many storm-bound gulls, all boats accounted for and none planning to go anywhere. The pilot boat lay in sheltered water at Westhaven, too, for the bar was in too great a fury to permit venturing further out to sea.

Out at sea, south and west of the shifting white geysers that marked the jetty's tip, an ocean steamship lay hove to. Captain Oscar Kullbom had made many voyages to Grays Harbor in command of the 10,000-ton Liberty ship *Yorkmar*. He had experienced nasty weather off the bar more than once, but he had never seen the equal of this howling, shrieking confusion. He had swung the *Yorkmar* in toward the entrance two days before, but when he got a good look at the bar and was informed by radio that the pilot boat couldn't reach his ship, he put about to wait offshore for a break in the weather.

The break hadn't come. If anything, the storm was worse than when the *Yorkmar* had made her landfall two days before. The big intercoastal lumber carrier was in ballast, riding high and wall-sided to the storm's blast. As the wind and seas increased their violence the ship became almost unmanageable, yawing wildly, giving more heed to the mighty push of the inshore gale than to the guidance of her straining rudder.

Near noon on December 8 the low, black clouds lifted momentarily as the deluge of rain slacked off to a sullen drizzle. Visibility was better than it had been at any time since the *Yorkmar* had arrived off Grays Harbor.

Captain Kullbom made a quick decision. He swung the engine room telegraph handle to *ahead—full*. The signal jangled in the engine room. The propeller blades of the high-riding Liberty bit hard against the gray water, beating it to foam as the black oil-smoke whipped from the funnel. Under a full head of steam, the *Yorkmar* smashed her way in toward the Grays Harbor bar. With just a bit of luck, a brief continuation of improved visibility, she could make it inside the jetty's shelter, pick up the pilot there, proceed up the Chehalis River to the mill dock at Aberdeen.

But the *Yorkmar's* luck was all bad that day. As the big freighter rolled and pitched toward the entrance, a black rain squall swept in from seaward to blot out everything a ship's length beyond her plunging bow. For ten minutes the squall hid their peril from the officers on the *Yorkmar's* bridge. Then it lifted as suddenly as it had come. The ship was nearly a mile off course, swept northward by wind and sea, heading straight for the massive, sea-swept rocks of the north jetty.

It was a desperate situation. The great man-made stone reef was coming up fast on the freighter's port bow. Every instinct prompted her master to swing her bow hard to starboard . . . away from the certain destruction that awaited her. But his sea knowledge told him that it was impossible. As she swung and came broadside to the storm she would inevitably be carried the few remaining yards that separated her from grinding rocks and boiling surf.

So, in a last desperate gamble, he turned his ship to port, hoping to swing her clear around and head back out to sea. It was a wise choice, and it almost succeeded. Turning in that direction, the gale gave added push to the ship's rudder, the clumsy Liberty ship fairly spinning around on her heel.

She came around with a little margin of safety. The jetty's seaward end was off her starboard beam; then it began to draw away astern. Just as it seemed that the captain's split-second decision was to pay off, the storm struck again at the struggling freighter.

A huge comber, a rolling, liquid mountain that dwarfed the great seas around it, came hissing in to take full control of the ship. The

jetty was cleared, but the *Yorkmar* was slammed helplessly on the open beach just to the north of it. Both anchors were dropped, but they slid helplessly, unable to get a grip in the smooth, packed sand. Succeeding breakers forced the ship solidly up broadside on the beach, the full length of her hull exposed to the sea.

The word spread fast that another ship had hit the beach at Grays Harbor. Shipping men shook their heads sadly, while beachcombers rubbed their hands in anticipation. It was a foregone conclusion that the freighter was doomed. Many ships had stranded along that stretch of coast; no big ship, once forced in broadside, had ever been refloated. Some of them sank from sight under the shifting sand. Most of them were battered to pieces by the hammering seas, their wreckage strewn for miles along the beach.

The only question in anyone's mind was which of these two ultimate fates awaited the *Yorkmar*. Captain Kullbom and his crew stayed aboard, kept there by the faintest flicker of hope that their ship could still be salvaged. Afterward they admitted that it was a very faint hope indeed. In their hearts they felt the ship was there to stay.

They saw no particular reason to feel more optimistic the next morning when a lop-sided looking little ship came plunging out of the storm to have a look at the wreck. As she lay tossing in the midst of the mile-wide breaker line that separated the stranded ship from the open sea, the new-comer looked capable and seaworthy enough, but hardly what was needed to pull a 10,000-ton freighter off a lee shore in the teeth of a December gale.

The little ship was the recently commissioned deep-sea salvage tug *Salvage Chief*, once a Navy LSM designed to land troops and equipment on the invasion beaches of World War II. Now she was a sea-going specialist, a ship designed for the primary purpose of rescuing other ships trapped on the grim shores of the North Pacific. She had come up from Astoria when word of the *Yorkmar's* plight reached there. This was her first real opportunity to prove whether or not she could do the sort of work she was built to do.

It would be a test for her owner, Columbia River salvage master Fred Devine, too. To him the *Salvage Chief* represented the savings of a lifetime and the realization of a dream of 20 years standing. Twenty years earlier, in December of 1932, Devine had watched the 8,800-

RIGHT IN THE BREAKERS, the mighty **Salvage Chief,** with heavy anchors out forward, begins working the stranded **Yorkmar** toward safety.

ton Hog Islander *Sea Thrush* fight for life on Clatsop Spit at the mouth of the Columbia.

Unassisted, the stranded freighter had worked her way through nearly 2000 feet of shifting sand toward deep water before her seams opened and her wreckage littered the inshore beaches. Devine was one of the crew that had boarded her, sealed her hatches, tried to devise some plan to help the stricken ship fight her way back to sea. There was no way, then, but Devine was sure that a way could be devised.

A ship, or even a barge, seaworthy enough to be anchored in the surf and equipped with winches powerful enough to keep a constant strain on the stranded freighter could have saved the *Sea Thrush*; could save other ships in similar straits.

In the years that followed Devine saw other ships and sea-going barges smashed to bits on the Oregon and Washington coast. He was sure

that he could have saved many of them if his salvage vessel were a reality instead of just a set of plans on paper.

When World War II came, Devine was in charge of diving crews in the Portland area shipyards. Supervising an 80-man crew, he managed a full eight hours of diving each working day as well. His dream of a perfect salvage ship was harnessed to everyday reality now, and it was moving fast toward fulfillment. He saved money, traded his work and knowledge for equipment that could be used to build his ship when the war was over.

The LSM hull that was to become the *Salvage Chief* was bought as government surplus in 1947. A year later the bare, undecked hull was moved to the Swan Island plant of Consolidated Builders for conversion. A fleet of worn out LSTs were being scrapped at the Consolidated yard that year. The ships were in poor condition, but much of their equipment

ONE OF THE SAL-VAGE CHIEF'S early rescue operations was the salvage of the sea-going tug **L. H. Cool-idge,** which stranded near Bandon, Oregon in 1949.

wasn't.

Six of their powerful winches, each able to pull 120 tons, were installed in the open hull of the LSM. Powerful diesel generators were shifted from the dead LSTs to the smaller ship which was undergoing a rebirth. Finally recut steel decking from the LSTs was installed over the machinery to give the *Salvage Chief* a new main deck.

Completed at last, the *Salvage Chief* was certainly unique in appearance. Built for highly specialized work, she was as unusual in her looks as in her trade. Her 203-foot steel hull, designed as a floating p l a t f o r m for salvage operations, was almost clear of the usual tug-boat superstructure. A narrow cylindrical steel deckhouse topped by pilot house and flying bridge amidships looked something like a sub-marine's conning tower, except that it was off-set on the tug's starboard side. An open, railed bridge extended from pilot house to the port gunwale, serving as a platform from which sal-vage operations could be directed. To the lay-man's eye the *Salvage Chief* was not a beautiful ship, but she looked mighty good to her owner. He had waited a long time for her, and she was exactly what he wanted.

The *Salvage Chief* was ready for business in 1949, but the kind of business Fred Devine needed to prove the worth of his theories and his ship just didn't turn up. A cannery tender slammed on the beach between the Columbia River and Willapa Harbor. The *Salvage Chief* yanked her off like a bulldozer towing a motor-scooter out of a mud puddle. But the tender

was a small ship, a converted LCT, and no real test of the *Chief's* strength. After that there were other small jobs; a loaded log barge pulled off the Oregon coast, a big tug refloated near Bandon, a big steel barge of the Puget Sound Tug and Barge fleet rescued from the beach near the Umpqua River bar. The *Salvage Chief* sailed north to pull the deep-laden barge *Kiska Island* from a rock reef on the Inside Passage of Alaska. She sailed south to refloat the coastal lumber schooner *Cynthia Olson* at Bandon. She put out the fatal fire that swept the Danish cargo liner *Erria* off Astoria in 1951.

The *Salvage Chief* found other jobs to do, but they were all relatively small jobs . . . until the *Yorkmar* struck.

There was no doubt in the minds of Devine and his 16-man crew that they had found their big job as the *Chief* slogged through the break-ers, easing in toward the stranded freighter. The 700-ton salvage tug was dwarfed by the great seas around her and by the 10,000-ton bulk of the stricken *Yorkmar* which lay like a huge stranded whale, high on the beach.

On shore, crowds had collected to view the doomed ship. Odds were 20 to one along the Grays Harbor waterfront that the *Yorkmar* would never leave the beach in one piece. The Coast Guard had rigged a breeches buoy from ship to beach, but the freighter's crew was stay-ing with her.

It was obvious to Devine, to the *Chief's* vet-eran skipper, Captain Vince Miller, to mate Ray Mattilla, to the tug's entire crew of expert seamen and technicians, that nothing could be

WITH THE RED STACK TUG SEA LION helping out in deep water, the **Salvage Chief,** in the breakers, hauls the stranded **Yorkmar** toward safety in one of the West Coast's most thrilling salvage operations.

done as long as the storm raged with its present fury. After a cautious survey, the *Chief* eased back out of the surf, swung offshore, and turned in to cross the bar. She tied up for the night in the quiet waters off Westport.

She put to sea again the next morning, but again the storm and the huge breakers drove her back to shelter. Not until the third day, December 11, was it possible to begin preliminary salvage operations. The storm was still hammering at sea and shore, but it was losing some of its maniacal fury.

The *Salvage Chief* nosed into the line of breakers, easing inshore under a dead slow bell. A mistake in judgment now could send her hurtling ashore to join the ship she was trying to save.

Two thousand yards offshore from the beached freighter the salvage tug hove to while a couple of big anchors splashed into the boiling surf. Then, as the steel anchor cables payed out slowly the *Chief* backed cautiously toward shore for another 800 yards. Then she brought up on the anchors, 1200 yards off the beach, her stern toward the *Yorkmar.*

The little ship jerked at her anchors like a maddened stallion, dipping her blunt bows viciously in the roaring surf, her stern veering wildly from side to side. Violent cross seas whipped up by the southwest wind fighting the northerly current scattered the incoming breakers in roaring confusion. In this chaos the men of the *Salvage Chief* fought to send a line from their Lyle gun to the *Yorkmar's* deck. Every attempt failed, the line breaking or fouling before a towing hawser could be bent on.

As a last resort a light line was floated ashore fastened to an empty oil drum. Coast Guardsmen carried the line to the freighter. Aboard the *Yorkmar,* crewmen made a heavier manila line fast. It was hauled back to the tug by hand as a precaution against its breaking under a sudden strain. A three quarter inch steel cable was drawn back aboard the *Yorkmar* on the end of the manila line. Finally a heavy steel towing cable was hauled back out by the *Chief's* powerful winches.

There was no time to rig additional lines between the two ships that day. All night the *Salvage Chief* hung on her two anchors in the pounding surf, the single line of hope stretching away in the darkness to link her with the stranded ship. In the morning one of the anchor cables parted. The other began to drag. The

Chief had been working with only six feet of water under her stern; now she was being driven into even shallower water. There was nothing for it but to cut the towing line to the *Yorkmar* and beat out to sea while she was still afloat. The backbreaking, dangerous work of the past 24 hours was all wasted effort now.

The *Salvage Chief* didn't return to the scene of her labors until December 16. Her crew hadn't been idle during the waiting period. Her winches carried 9000 feet of new, heavy tow line and she carried two giant salvage anchors weighing five tons each, borrowed from the Bremerton Navy Yard.

A crew of expert riggers—many of them recruited from Grays Harbor logging camps—had arrived to prepare the *Yorkmar* for the next effort. Some of them went aboard by breeches buoy. Others stayed on the sand to rig beach gear . . . heavy anchors attached to the freighter's steam winches to enable her to add her own power to the tug's mighty pull.

On December 18 all preparations had been made. The wind and seas had subsided to their normal winter unpleasantness, and two towing lines were stretched between freighter and tug well before noon. The time element was important, for an 11.9-foot tide, one of the year's highest, was due at noon that day.

For an hour the *Salvage Chief's* powerful diesels rumbled at full throttle, the taut tow lines vibrating under the strain of the steady pull. Then, as the tide neared its flood, the great bulk of the freighter trembled and stirred in the sand. The movement increased, the ship's stern literally bouncing over the packed beach until it was pointed almost directly out to sea. The ship was no longer helplessly broadside to the shore and the breakers.

Steam was up in the freighter's boilers and as the stern swung around into deeper water her huge propeller was set to turning, the churning of the blades clearing out sand to make a seaward path, the vibration of their turning helping to break the beach's grip on the great hull.

Stern-first, the *Yorkmar* moved ponderously toward deep water. Then the ebbing tide deserted her to leave her still solidly beached. She was 200 feet closer to salvation . . . or to a broken back. It all depended on what happened between then and the arrival of the next—and last—11.9-foot tide on December 18.

Until that tide came the *Salvage Chief* kept a constant pull on the towing lines. If it gained nothing it at least minimized the possibility of losing everything that had been gained already.

When the time for the final effort arrived the *Salvage Chief* had a lot of company. Offshore the Coast Guard cutters *McLane* and *Balsam* were standing by. Further in, but in deep water outside the breaker line lay the big Red Stack tug *Sea Lion*. She had a 1200-foot line fast to the *Salvage Chief's* bow to add her weight to the big pull, but it was mostly the *Chief's* show; the *Chief's* and Fred Devine's. It was a show that would be the pay-off on a dream of 20 year's standing, or a complete fiasco. There was no half-way ground in this struggle.

At a few minutes after noon Devine called the *Sea Lion* by radio. At his word the big San Francisco tug's engines roared to full throttle. The *Salvage Chief* trembled to the wide-open thrust of her own mighty diesels. Tow lines rose dripping from the sea.

Six minutes later Devine called the *Sea Lion* again. She could shut down her engines. The *Yorkmar* was afloat.

Pausing only long enough to haul in two of her big anchors and abandon the third, the *Salvage Chief* ramped four miles out to sea, the resurrected freighter following obediently, stern-first. Then her own engines took over and a triumphal procession . . . the *Yorkmar*, *Balsam*, *McLane*, *Sea Lion*—and *Salvage Chief* —headed south toward the Columbia River entrance.

At Portland the *Yorkmar* was checked over and given minor repairs. Her bottom plates were pushed upward where she had rested on the beach, but she was sound enough to pick up her lumber cargo and return to the East Coast for final repairs to her hull.

Not long ago the writer watched the Liberty ship *Yorkmar* swing in past the Grays Harbor jetties, riding high and headed for the mill dock at Aberdeen. She looked like any of a hundred of her mass-produced sisters of the wartime merchant fleet. It was a routine crossing of the bar, but on her bridge her captain . . . cleared of all blame for her stranding . . . must have been thinking of the one time she didn't make it. She made maritime history then; the only ocean ship ever to go where she went and live to sail again.

She lived because a squat, powerful Northwest tugboat named *Salvage Chief* was there to give her a fighting chance for life. That's something no ship beached on the Northwest Coast has ever had before. There was a lot of solid substance after all in the twenty year old dream of Fred Devine, salvage master.

RESCUE

The *Salvage Chief* hasn't been resting on her laurels since she amazed the experts by yanking the *Yorkmar*, almost undamaged, off the Grays Harbor beach. Twelve days after her return to Astoria Captain Miller was taking her back across the bar in the teeth of a new 60 mile an hour storm. Out off the Columbia River lightship she picked up the Liberian Liberty Ship *Venerator*, out of fuel and manned by an anxious crew who hoped her anchors would hold.

As midnight ushered in another year, 1953, the *Salvage Chief* was rumbling up the Columbia River on the safe side of the bar, the steamship *Venerator* following quietly in her wake. The Pacific Graveyard had lost another prospective victim, while Fred Devine's mighty *Salvage Chief* was celebrating the New Year in the most fitting manner possible.

The big Astoria salvage tug wasn't the only unit of the Pacific Northwest workboat fleet to observe the holiday season by a victory over the sea. Up at Vancouver, British Columbia, a pair of storm-battered ships eased into the harbor at about the time people ashore were sweeping up the rumpled gift wrappings and thinking about untrimming the Christmas tree. The two ships were the 10,000-ton Canadian-Pacific freighter *Maplecove* and the 435-ton deep sea tug *Island Sovereign* of the Island Tug and Barge Company. The date was December 27, 1952, and to the men on these two ships Christmas had been just another short day and long night spent fighting huge seas and mighty winds.

Three days before Christmas the *Maplecove* was in the mid-Pacific, rolling and pitching toward Vancouver on a return voyage from Yokohama. Winds of nearly hurricane force clawed at the ship as she plunged through sweeping seas as high as a four-story building.

It was nasty going, but the ship's master, Captain R. A. Leicester, and his 62-man crew weren't particularly worried. As staunch and seaworthy a ship as the *Maplecove* had little to fear from a mid-Pacific gale. She was behaving well, her powerful engines steaming smoothly. There was a good chance that, in spite of the howling storm, she would make the 1200 miles to her home port in time to put her crew ashore for Christmas.

Then, suddenly and quite without warning, the ship yawed wildly from her course, falling off before the wind to wallow sickeningly in the trough of the seas. The quartermaster on watch spun the wheel hard over, but there was no response. In a matter of minutes it was clear enough that something serious had happened to the ship's steering mechanism. There was no way to make her answer her helm. The storm was getting worse.

There was no way of knowing it then, but the ship's great steel rudder was no longer swinging beneath the overhang of the stern. The smashing waves had torn it off bodily, leaving only a few inches of jagged metal where it should have been.

Captain Leicester directed the rigging of a jury rudder fashioned from ladders, steel gratings and odds and ends of canvas, but it was

LEAVING S.S. MAPLECOVE resting at her berth in Vancouver Harbour, **Island Sovereign** pulls away after completion of epic towing feat in the stormy Pacific—December 27, 1952.—(Photo courtesy Island Tug and Barge, Ltd.)

completely ineffective a g a i n s t the power of wind and sea. The veteran shipmaster could find only one thing in his favor; the wind that screamed around his vessel was wild and unpredictable, but it was, for the most part, blowing in the direction he wanted to go. Perhaps he could make use of the gales that seemed to be trying to overwhelm the *Maplecove.*

Progress was being made, however erratic and frustrating it might seem, and two United States Coast Guard cutters had responded to the freighter's radio call for assistance. Things could be worse.

More help was on the way, too, as soon as the *Maplecove's* radio message was flashed to her operators in British Columbia. In less than an hour the tug *Island Sovereign* headed out of Vancouver harbor for Victoria to pick up additional men and equipment. Hours before dawn the next morning she was racing down the strait toward the storm-wracked ocean.

The *Island Sovereign,* a new-comer to the North Coast towing fleets, is a handsome little ship by any standards, and big by tugboat standards. Built in Chicago for the U.S. Army as the LT-62 in 1944, the 123-foot craft was

salvaged from the rocky shore of Seymour Narrows to be converted to a sleek civilian. When the job was finished a number of die-hard tugboaters looked her over critically, averring that she was "too danged glamorous for a tugboat." Now she was going to prove that she was rugged as well as handsome.

She started proving it as soon as she nosed out past Cape Flattery to face the full blast of the storm. It was fortunate that quartermaster Ken Wallace was well braced at the wheel for, as he put it, "she started diving." After that, days and hours became blurred and vague to the men of the *Island Sovereign.* In the words of her master, Captain Art Warren, "It was just one long day to us. The gales never slackened and before one would finish, another would begin."

That was on Friday, and Monday saw the tug still smashing through ever - increasing seas, stubbornly holding her west-southwest course toward the *Maplecove.* Life aboard the tug had been a prolonged hell of wet and cold and hunger and sleeplessness. Sullen green seas crashed over the bows to sweep clear across the superstructure and pilot house. Veteran coasting

ISLAND SOVEREIGN towing Greek-owned Panamanian freighter **Adamas** which ran out of fuel 500 miles west of Victoria. Despite rough seas and 60 mile gales, **Sovereign** towed **Adamas** safely into Victoria, November 19, 1955.—(Photo courtesy Island Tug and Barge, Ltd.)

master Charles Scholes, who had signed on for the voyage as mate and navigator, was sent hurtling across the pilot house to crash in a heap on the deck. It looked as if his swollen arm might be broken, but there was no time to worry about it. He kept working.

There was no hot food and no rest. Men off watch tried tying themselves in their sodden bunks, but there was no way of securing themselves against the awful gyrations of the tug. She was literally standing on her head.

Then a radio message was received from the Coast Guard weather ship *St. Catherine* on station further out at sea:

Forty foot waves and 80-mile gales approaching. Strongly advise you return to Cape Flattery.

It was excellent advice, but there was now a 650-mile expanse of insane ocean between the *Island Sovereign* and that shelter. She made it back to western Vancouver Island to ride out the worst of the storm's climax off the mouth of historic Nootka Sound. Unbelievably, it was worse than it had been at sea. The tug rolled 45, 50, at times as far as 55 degrees, lying almost on her side, with her 15-foot high navigating bridge dipping into the sea. Solid, green water smashed over her pilot house.

Icy water seeped inside the hull and deck-houses. Men who had spent their lives at sea were violently sick. Down in the engine room a compressor broke bathing engineers Vadim Stavrokov and Bill Frost with oil. Engineer Stavrokov was a veteran of Sir Hubert Wilkin's 1913 submarine expedition to the Arctic, but that had been a tame affair compared to this. On Christmas day the cook, working heroically in his flooded galley, produced a pot of stew. It was thin and watery, but it was hot—the first hot food the crew had tasted that voyage—and the cook received their blessings.

The *Maplecove*, in the meantime, was still making her erratic progress toward the coast. Things aboard the 10,000-tonner were far more pleasant than on the tug that was trying to rescue her. As a matter of fact, she was in far less actual danger. The first of the Coast Guard cutters had arrived in the freighter's vicinity and was standing by. The *St. Catherine*, heading that way when it was clear that the *Island Sovereign* was stopped, returned to her weather station when she received word of the cutter's arrival.

When the full fury of the storm began to abate a little the battered *Island Sovereign* made new arrangements to meet the *Maple-*

DEEP-SEA TUG AGNES FOSS

cove. Captain Leicester's stop-and-go technique was working out well and the disabled steamship was working her way steadily in. The two ships finally met 55 miles west of Swiftsure lightship off the Washington coast.

Swooping high and dropping low on swells that still rose 20 feet or more, the tug worked in to within 50 feet of the plunging freighter but a hand line thrown from the heaving deck still fell short of the big ship's rail. Then a line-carrying rocket was fired from the freighter toward the tug to chalk up another narrow escape for a member of the *Island Sovereign's* crew. The rocket struck the tug's deckhouse a foot from the head of deckhand Bill Bean. The rocket's b o o s t e r charge, unexpended at such close range, exploded as it struck.

But luck was still with the tugboat men. Bean wasn't hurt, and a line at last connected the *Maplecove* and the *Island Sovereign.* True, it was a thin and tenuous line at first, but as the freighter's crew hauled away manfully, it was followed by manila rope, then by a heavy hawser, and, finally, by a steel towing line. The storm was still too wild to permit men to work on the tug's exposed deck, so the lines had to be manhandled in through the seamen's quarters and galley to the half-flooded towing room and out over the stern.

The operation was completed just in time, for it was getting dark and another all-out storm was headed for the coast. It was no place for a rudderless freighter on a lee shore. But the *Island Sovereign* had taken over and things were under control at last. Just as darkness

shut in the big tug swung around to haul the dripping line from the sea and start the *Maplecove* toward the shelter of Cape Flattery.

The new storm caught tug and tow before they got in, but nothing could bother them much after what they had been through already. A couple of hours after midnight the two ships were anchored in English Bay, off Vancouver harbor, waiting for the tide. At 7:30 on the morning of December 27 the *Island Sovereign* was proudly helping the big *Maplecove* into her berth at the Canadian Pacific dock. The ordeal was over and *Island Sovereign* had proven that good looks in a tug are no bar to strength and stamina.

Of course the *Agnes Foss* could swap yarns with her and not come off second best. Their conversation would make a fine subject for Rudyard Kipling, who loved to write about the imaginary talk of mechanical things like railway locomotives and automobiles and ships.

Kipling would probably have the gracefully streamlined *Island Sovereign* looking haughtily down her hause-pipes at the rangy Yankee tug while murmuring superciliously through her uptakes, "But you just haven't seen a *real* s t o r m, my dear; not like the one *I* fought through to get my line to the *Maplecove.*"

And while an old ferry boat tied up in the background rubbed her worn strakes against a piling, wailing *"Aiyeee"* and muttering of the pain of sprung frames suffered in 40 years of being butted into slips by clumsy pilots, the *Agnes* would no doubt snort a great snort of disgust from her fat green and white funnel

GREEK FREIGHTER MAKEDONIA, disabled in the mid-Pacific, was saved from probable disaster by the Island Tug and Barge Company's mighty **Sudbury.** In the words of the Vancouver **Province** Marine Editor, Norman Hacking, it was "one of the great feats of the sea."

and sulk a while. But, being a lady, she couldn't keep quiet long.

"When you've been buttin' yer head against the ocean as long as *I* have," she'd rumble, "y' may learn enough at least to be quiet 'til yer spoken to when docked alongside yer betters. A fancy jade you may be, wi' yer shiny paint an' yer fancy bridgework, but I'll thank you to remember I'm bigger than you and for all yer fancy superchargers and suchlike gadgets I'm powerfuller than you . . . and I was sailin' the seas when the folks that built you was sailin' toy boats in mud puddles."

Then, nodding emphatically in the swell of a passing Princess liner, the *Agnes Foss* might tell of *her* latest bout with the North Pacific; of the time she went out to pick up the derelict steamship *Margo.*

It was less than a year after the *Island Sovereign's* big adventure that the *Margo,* a 10,000-ton freighter of Panamanian registry ran into trouble. Headed for Portland from the Orient, she was fighting heavy gales and high seas like those that had smashed the *Maplecove's* rudder the year before. She was just about as far from the American coast as the Canadian freighter had been, too, when it happened. Some 1250 miles off the Washington coast, the *Margo* lost her propeller.

It was well that she had plenty of sea-room

when her propeller snapped off and dropped to the bottom of the ocean, for she began drifting helplessly toward the shores of the Northwest Coast at a rate of 5 knots. Since she was in no immediate danger, her owners began negotiations with Pacific Northwest towing firms on a competitive bid basis. The job was awarded to the Foss Launch and Tug Company on November 14, 1953.

There is never time for long delays when a ship is drifting out of control in mid-winter storms. Too many things can happen. A tug had to be dispatched at once, and the *Agnes Foss,* best readily available boat for this sort of work, was lying at the company's Seattle moorings.

She hadn't been there long. Only the day before the sea-stained *Agnes* had come back from a 50-day voyage to Icy Bay, Alaska. Hauling oil drilling equipment to the unprotected gulf, the big tug had battled Arctic gales there in addition to sweating out the round-trip through the treacherous I n s i d e Passage and around the frigid northern coast of Alaska.

Captain Vince Miller and the rest of her 15-man crew were enjoying a well-earned rest at home. They were just getting used to being warm and dry on a steady floor when they got the word that they were to run another little errand . . . a thousand miles out on an angry

133

ocean.

They wouldn't have been tugboat men if they hadn't engaged in some awesome cussing when they got the word. And they wouldn't have been tugboat men if they hadn't been ready to go a bit ahead of schedule. Six hours after the orders were received the *Agnes Foss* had been refueled, had taken on provisions enough to see her through an ocean voyage of indefinite length and, with her full crew aboard, was headed down-sound toward the Pacific.

The tug's best feature, as far as her crew was concerned, was her solid steel construction and enclosed working space. Even the towing machinery is enclosed in a relatively weather-proof room reached by inside passageways, so there was no need to venture out on the open decks. It would have been impossible to do so during most of the voyage, for they were swept by solid green seas almost continually.

But in spite of their ship's good points, the crew of the *Agnes Foss* were not embarked on a sea-going picnic. When the low, rangy boat plunged out of the shelter of Cape Flattery into the open sea she looked more like a submarine than a tugboat. The great gray seas swept clear over her, and her speed had to be lowered to seven knots. Even her rugged frame could not have withstood the battering of higher speed through such waves.

She left the strait on Sunday, November 15, and she didn't reach the drifting *Margo* until the following Friday. She was fighting every mile of the way. Huge seas lifting her stern made her almost impossible to steer sometimes, but ingenuity is part of the tugboat man's emergency equipment. A heavy anchor chain was trailed over the stern and its drag steadied the laboring tug, making it possible to hold her on course.

The wind varied in force, but only from high to higher. It never blew less than a full gale, at times approached hurricane force. During one 24-hour period the *Agnes Foss* logged only 170 miles, but she never faltered in her westward course. At last, on Friday, the 20th, two blips were picked up on the tug's radar screen. They were the *Margo* and the Coast Guard cutter *Koiner*, which had left her offshore weather station to stand by until the tug's arrival. Later that night the drifting ship's lights were sighted.

For three days the storm raged with unabated fury. Two more cutters arrived during that time; the *Finch* and the huge tug *Yocona*, but they were helpless to do anything except hang on and watch.

Then, late Monday evening, the wind moderated abruptly. It was still no mill-pond in the vicinity of the little flotilla. The wind blew steadily at 20 miles an hour and seas still ran 20 feet high, but compared to what it had been, this was balmy weather. Early the next morning the *Agnes Foss* went into action. Swinging in alongside the derelict freighter, her Lyle gun sent a line whistling across the big ship's deck. It was safely secured, to be followed by a heavy manila hawser. Then came a length of the tug's

TUGS OFFICIATE at the retirement and destruction of the former passenger liner **Southern Cross.** As the naval transport **Wharton,** the former trans-Atlantic liner is shown (below left) being moved down Seattle's Duwamish waterway toward a wrecking yard. Her upperworks removed, (below right) the remains of the **Wharton** are moved on toward a drydock, where the hull will be cut up for scrap. To the left in this picture is Joe Williamson's harbor launch, **Susan Jane,** from which many of the pictures in this book were taken.

134

MID-PACIFIC. The **Hercules** looked like this from the deck of her fleet-mate, **Monarch,** as they towed the hulk of the bombed battleship **Oklahoma** from Pearl Harbor toward San Francisco. Shortly after the two tugs were being dragged toward the depths of the Pacific by the sinking **Oklahoma.** Their escape was a maritime miracle.

big anchor cable made fast to the steel tow line.

Fifteen minutes after the Lyle gun banged out its single shot the lines were secured and the *Agnes Foss* had squared away for the long tow home. It wasn't as long as the outward run had been, for the ships had, by now, drifted to within 850 miles of the Oregon coast. But it was still a considerable distance, especially in view of the fact that the storm was soon back in full cry after its brief lull. But the tug had the only break she'd asked for: an opportunity to get her line aboard the disabled freighter. She drummed her way eastward at a steady five to six knot speed.

She paused only once in her steady progress, and that was only for long enough to shift the anchor chain which was being used to secure the tow line to the freighter. The massive steel links were wearing thin from the constant friction of the wildly pitching tow.

Midnight, Saturday, November 28, found tug and tow hove to off the Columbia River entrance to take aboard the bar pilots. Early the next morning the tow was transferred to the *Salvage Chief* for the final run upriver to Portland. The *Agnes Foss* was back at her Seattle

moorings the next day, and her worn-out crew looked her over sadly as they reached the dock. They'd spent the return voyage from Icy Bay giving her a shiny green and white paint job from stack lip to bulwarks. The new paint had been battered off in huge patches by the North Pacific rollers, and she looked as rusty and battered as any uncared for sea-tramp.

They had the whole job to do over again. But first there would be a few lovely, quiet days at home . . . unless the *Agnes* received another emergency call.

Oh, yes. In case you've been wondering, the Captain Vince Miller who took the *Agnes Foss* out to rescue the *Margo* was the same Captain Vince Miller who skippered the *Salvage Chief* during her amazing rescue of the *Yorkmar.*

Other crew members on the *Agnes Foss* that voyage were mates Joseph Le Blanch and Martin Connett, engineers Jack Gilden, Dexter Mc-Daniel and Alden Anderson, deck hands Morris Chayter, Saron Kvamshoim, W. Williams and Don Arthur, oilers John Holzbauer, George Scott and Jim McGinn, and, in the steward's department, Cliff Goodrich and S. Carey, Jr.

Real tugboat men, all.

CHANGING TIMES

The diesel engine, which has given new life to so many of the old steam towboats, spelled retirement and eventual destruction for some of them. A new heavy duty diesel costs a great many thousands of dollars, so owners who can afford them still have to think twice about their investment. It's hardly worth while to put that much money in a boat unless the hull is pretty certain to last as long as the engine. If there's any doubt about it the old steamer usually ends up in the bone yard.

Other small operators, unable to afford diesel conversion and losing money trying to compete against more economically powered boats, were forced to sell their steamers for what they could get. Those that didn't find buyers in the live boat market were offered to the junk dealers.

A number of people, particularly steamboat fans, will tell you that the great advantages of diesel power over steam in the realm of economy of operation are largely artificial; that they result from arbitrary government regulations rather than any real mechanical advantages on the part of the internal combustion rigs. There is considerable logic to back up their arguments.

Let's say you're operating a 75-foot steam tug. Government regulations require you to hire a seven man crew to operate her. She has to have a licensed master or mate in the pilot house, a licensed engineer below. She has to undergo frequent, t h o r o u g h and expensive Coast Guard inspections. She's a steamboat and she's subject to all the vast maze of steamboat inspection regulations that have accumulated in more than a century of bureaucracy.

So you get disgusted, pull out the engine and boiler, cut several feet off the top of the smokestack, and connect up a diesel. Now the government loses all interest in your business. You can run the boat all by yourself, if you feel up to it, or sign your Aunt Mehitable on as skipper, whether she has master's papers or not. The exhaustive inspections are a thing of the past; so are the resulting expensive refits that the government always seemed to feel were required, whether you agreed or not.

The old steam engine may have been running smoothly after half a century of hard work and showing no signs of wear. The new diesel may thump, emit evil smells, and require frequent maintenance, but the fact remains that the conversion has saved you money in future operating costs that probably mean the difference between profit and loss.

Tugboats have to operate at a profit, so the old steamers either get new engines or go out of business. The trend started along about 1925 and gained such momentum that a steam tug is almost as great a rarity as a full-rigged ship in Pacific Northwest waters nowadays. Some very colorful old characters got pushed aside in the shuffle.

One was the *Prospector*, last of the woodburning steamboats. Built at Seattle in 1898, she operated out of Olympia for many years as part of Captain Volney C. F. Young's Capital City Tug Company fleet. Her boiler fires had been fed by both coal and fuel oil at various times, but in her last years she went back to burning slabwood. There was something homely and friendly about the old *Prospector* as she

STEAM TUGS PROSPECTOR AND LUMBERMAN rest from their labors at Percival's Dock in Olympia. The **Prospector,** a wood-burner, did not survive the change from steam to diesel power. The **Lumberman,** thoroughly modernized, works for the Samson Tug and Barge Company of Sitka, Alaska.

clanked slowly up Budd Inlet in front of a long boom of logs, her fire wood stacked handily alongside her lower deckhouse where the fireman could reach it easily. The tang of wood smoke from her tall funnel was a pleasant change from oil fumes and she possessed a mellow double-chime whistle that was music to the ears.

Olympia's port was dredged out to provide safe mooring for deep-draft ocean ships in 1926, a development which provided the picturesque *Prospector* with a new job. She used to fuss importantly down to Doffelmyer Point, hail incoming freighters with a blast from her musical whistle, and lead them proudly into port by means of a hawser attached to their noses. Then she would help them swing around in the turning basin, nudge them against the dock, and go clanking off to other tasks, puffing clouds of fragrant wood smoke as she went.

When business slacked off in the 1930's Captain Young had the *Prospector* hauled out on the beach at Eld Inlet to rest while the diesel boats *Edward A. Young, Virjo Young* and *Mizpah* carried on the company's business. The old steamer caught on fire while she lay abandoned. When the fire burned out there was nothing left of her but a few charred ribs. She wasn't a big boat or a famous boat, but she had a lot of personality and those who knew her were sorry to see her go.

Her little fleet-mate, *Mizpah,* survived the change-over from steam to diesel. Captain Young launched her as a passenger and freight steamboat in 1905. Her keel had been laid on the same Friday that President McKinley was assassinated in 1901, but she lay unfinished for a long time until the hull was bought by Captain Young and engineer John C. Ross. She finally made her trial run on a Friday in 1905, making her maiden voyage on her regular route a Friday or two later.

She carried passengers, freight and mail between Olympia and Kamilche, stopping along the way at Hunter's Point, Little Skookum, and Oyster Bay points. Like most of the little in-

137

land steamboats of her day, she was very obliging and would make additional stops wherever a prospective customer might flag her down.

With Captain Young as skipper, pilot, purser and business agent and John Ross as engineer, wiper and water-tender, the little *Mizpah* worked up a profitable trade along her modest route. But things kept happening to her on Fridays. Engineer Ross was lost overboard and drowned in Oyster Bay on a Friday in 1906. Then, on a Friday in 1915, she caught on fire and burned to the water's edge. She was rebuilt as a tug after the fire, keeping her 75 horsepower compound steam engine until 1922. Then

COMING ALONGSIDE a lumber scow, Capt. Volney Young's little tug **Mizpah** looks as if she had always been in the towing business, but more than half a century ago she had freight and passenger decks, was powered by a compound steam engine and ran on the Olympia-Kamilche mail route.

DIESEL ENGINES, like this one in the **Foss 18,** brought a new lease on life to scores of old steam tugs. The **Foss 18** was once the steam tug **Alice,** built in 1892.

she got an early model Fairbanks-Morse diesel to become one of the first motor tugs on upper Puget Sound.

When a destructive hurricane hit Puget Sound on a Friday in 1934 the *Mizpah* was bound to get mixed up in it. She did, sinking from a terrific battering received in line of duty. She recovered from this misadventure to go on working as a harbor tug and general towboat and at last reports her 1922-model diesel engine was still in good condition. This might appear to be a blow to steamboat fans, but they can always point out that *Mary D. Hume's* steam engine was still working fine when it was pulled out—and its an 1881-model.

Most of the tugboats around Olympia and upper Puget Sound were still using their steam engines when the *Mizpah* switched over to diesel, but one exception was the handsome little *Sandman*, built at Crawford and Reid's yard in 1910. She was equipped with a heavy-duty gasoline engine which was a step removed from the semi-diesels that came a little later. The *Sandman* had to postpone her debut while her revolutionary new engine was on display at Seattle's Alaska-Yukon-Pacific Exposition. Then she chugged up the sound to Olympia, from which port she has operated ever since.

During the first 20 years or so of her career she was dressed in gleaming white paint from waterline to jaunty buff funnel. Door and window frames were touched up with natural wood varnish. Combined with her graceful Crawford and Reid lines, this gave her the look of a yacht rather than a tugboat and she had many admirers. She's lost some of her glamour in recent years; her black hull paint and buff deckhouse don't set off her trim lines to best advantage, but it's the standard color of Delta Smyth's tugboat fleet. It's a good deal more practical than the old color scheme, too. And nobody mistakes the little *Sandman* for a yacht any more.

Most of the old steam tugs that snorted scornfully at the new-fangled little boats like *Mizpah* and *Sandman* have long since followed their lead. Those that didn't have followed the old *Prospector's* trail to oblivion. People who knew them in the old days would have trouble recognizing them since they have gone modern. The *Harold C.*, built at Ballard in 1903, used to have a bright orange deckhouse and a black, skinny steamboat funnel. Now she's the *Foss 17*, a typical, compact diesel harbor tug. The old *Alice* is the *Simon Foss* now, having undergone much the same changes as the *Harold C.* It's an old story for *Alice,* though. She was built in 1897 as a passenger steamboat, was later cut down as a steam tug, and was trimmed a bit further to assume the typical lines of a modern motorized towboat.

One of the few that might still be recognized is Delta Smyth's old steamer *Olympian,* built at Tacoma in 1898. She's the *Adeline Foss* now, the only steam tug left in the big Foss fleet, but it's an unprofitable distinction. She's been dozing away at her moorings for several years now, her boiler cold and her useful life apparently over . . . unless Dr. Diesel gives her a shot in the arm.

You will run across the rejuvenated old steamboats all over Puget Sound, but unless you are very familiar with them, you won't be able to tell them from the more modern boats. The 45 year old S.S. *Forest T. Crosby* looks young and trim as Washington Tug and Barge Company's M.S. *Reliance.* The old Cary-Davis steamer *Katahdin* doesn't show her age (she's nearly 60) as the diesel *Catherine Foss.* The little sound passenger steamer *Audrey,* built in 1909, still has her original name but she's a diesel towboat now, too, hauling log booms and fuel barges at Olympia.

If you take the time to total up the average ages of the boats operated by an average Puget Sound towing company you'll probably come up with a figure of somewhere around 40 years. That's figuring in the big new offshore boats, most of them built during the World War II period. Which makes it pretty obvious that a lot of the tugs have outlived the age of steam by adapting themselves to changed conditions.

Probably hardest hit by the transition were the old passenger steamers. When highway and railway competition began to make their old routes unprofitable their owners looked around for new jobs to keep them busy. Many of the bigger steamboats compromised with the automobiles by becoming ferry boats. Even splendid stern-wheel packets like the *Bailey Gatzert* and *Telephone* made the change, thereby extending their lives for a while. Smaller steamboats, not capable of hauling enough automobiles to make profitable ferries, turned to towing.

Most of them were getting on in years when they became tugboats. Worth rebuilding once, most of them fell by the wayside when their owners were faced with the heavy expense of another conversion—to diesel power. Another point against them was their hull construction. Most of them were built on long, slim lines

with knifelike bows and low freeboard. This was fine in the day of the passenger steamboat, which was a competitive age, for it gave them the speed needed to outrace rivals and garner the cream of the passenger and freight business.

Unfortunately this design, ideal for racing passenger steamboats, was the opposite of ideal for salt water towboats. They need a broad, deep, high-bowed hull under them to give them the stability and seaworthiness they need. They need heavy timbers to withstand the bruises and shocks that are occupational hazards in their business. The little passenger steamers were built light and limber to give them the high speed that, as tugboats, they no longer needed.

The slim little *Magnolia* was an example of the lightly graceful passenger boats that tried

STEAMER ADVANCE once proudly sailed between Seattle and Dogfish Bay. Later, shown below, she became a diesel tug. Finally, worn out despite her many face-liftings, she was burned during the finale of a Seafair celebration in Seattle.

EVEN WHEN SHE WAS NEW, in 1895, the government steamer **Wigwam** wasn't noted for speed, but the **Foss 19** has been a frequent winner of tugboat races in recent years. It takes a skilled eye to note any similarity between the **Wigwam** (below) and the **Foss 19** (above), but they are one and the same craft . . . an interesting example of tugboat transformation.

their hand at tugboating. She was 101 feet long with a beam of just over 18 feet, while her gross tonnage was measured at just 57 tons. The trend has been steadily in the opposite direction. Puget Sound Tug's *Tyee*, built in 1927 as the *Crowley No. 28* is only 80 feet long, but her beam is 20 feet and she registers 75 gross tons. American Tugboat Company's powerful little harbor tug *Peter* isn't much more than half the old *Magnolia's* length, but her width is only a foot less and her tonnage is the same. She was built in 1937. Foss Launch and Tug Company's welded steel *Brynn Foss*, launched in 1952, is 72 feet long, 21 feet beam, 102 gross tons.

As a passenger steamer piloted by Captain Fred Sutter, the first little *Magnolia* gained a reputation as a racer which was outstanding in an era and an area where steamboat racing was a favorite pastime. Her greatest fame was gained in her battle with Captain Chance Wyman's *Vashon* on the Tacoma-Quartermaster Harbor route. Competition became so spirited that passengers on the rival steamboats began to fear for their lives, finally banding together to force a cessation of hostilities. After that the *Magnolia* operated as a direct boat between Seattle and Olympia. She remained in this trade until the early 1920's; was the last scheduled passenger steamer to serve Olympia, which had been a steamboat port since 1853.

She lost none of her slim good looks when she became a towboat for the Olson Tugboat Company at Tacoma. The Olson colors—white touched up with scarlet trim—set her off to good advantage. Under Captain Paddy Craig she worked hard at log and barge towing for some 15 years, but she just wasn't built for the work. It was like hitching a dainty race horse to a brewery wagon, and it wore her out. When the towing fleet went diesel the *Magnolia* was dismantled, a new little diesel tug carrying on her name in the Olson fleet.

There were a number of others. The *Advance*, which began her career as a passenger steamboat at Poulsbo in 1899, also worked as an Olson tug, but she ended her days as a public spectacle in 1951. As the traditional "Neptune's Barge", she was burned by the villianous Davy Jones to provide a climax to Seattle's Seafair of that year. The old Hood Canal steamboat *Lydia Thompson*, built at Port Angeles in 1893, became the steam tug *Monitor*. The little Lake Washington steamer *Lady of the Lake* was converted to a tug named *Ruth*. *Concordia, Kenai, Mercer, Norwood, Prosper, Urania*—these and many more of the old time steamboats tried their hands at towing for a while, but only a few of them have survived.

A lot of the Puget Sound stern-wheelers ended up toting barges and log booms too. It was a simple matter for them, requiring only a towing engine down on the boiler deck to put them in business.

Some of them, like the fast little Olympia-Shelton paddler *S. G. Simpson* and the old Grays Harbor packet *City of Aberdeen*, stayed on Puget Sound. The *Simpson*, built in 1907 for the Shelton Transportation Company, was pushed out of the passenger business by highway competition in 1925. After that she worked for a while as a Puget Sound Freight Lines cargo carrier, but in this business too, the fine lines and fast engines of a passenger boat were a liability rather than an asset.

She was sold to Martin Tjerne of Stanwood in 1928, being rebuilt at Everett as the towboat *E. G. English*. Skippered by Captain Henry Whalen, she towed logs between the Skagit River and Camano Island until the early 1940's.

THE SLIM MAGNOLIA (above) was originally a fast-stepping passenger steamer. The chunky **Tyee** (below) was built as a diesel tug. The hull lines of the two boats tell their story.

THE GLEANER, built at Bandon, Oregon in 1908, was a new boat when this picture was taken. She was bringing the lumber schooner **Sadie** across the Umpqua River Bar, with the lighthouse tender **Heather** following astern.

IN GOVERNMENT SERVICE as the ST-216, the old Gleaner did World War II towing jobs from San Francisco to the Bering Sea.

Then progress caught up with her at last and she was shoved ashore on a bend of the Skagit, her slim hull buried under tons of rocks and gravel.

The *City of Aberdeen* was built on Grays Harbor in 1891 to run on the Chehalis River, but early in her career she made a brief ocean voyage to enter the Puget Sound passenger trade. She spent most of her time paddling sedately between Seattle, Tacoma and Olympia, but was known, upon occasion, to catch the racing fever. She once took on the famed Portland-built stern-wheeler *Greyhound* and beat her. It was difficult to tell who was most amazed at the outcome—the crew of the *Greyhound* or the *Aberdeen's* men.

This was one of the few old time Sound steamboat races of which an authentic eyewitness description survives. Engineer Nick Perring, of Olympia, was in charge of the *Aberdeen's* power plant when the big race was staged. He began steamboating on the original *Goliah* in the 1870's and retired after World War I when the passenger steamer *Nisqually*, on which he was chief, changed her name to *Astorian* and moved down to the lower Columbia. Engineer Perring was alert and interested in steamboating until his death in 1949. In his

later years he was interviewed by the late Jim Bashford, marine editor of the Tacoma *News-Tribune*. This is his own account of the *Aberdeen's* fabled race with the *Greyhound*:

"That was quite a race. Old man Willey (the boat's owner) came aboard one day and asked me if I could beat the Greyhound *with the* Aberdeen. *I told him I could, provided I was allowed to have the say in loading the Aberdeen. She was a deceiving outfit when it came to speed. To run she had to be trimmed just right. I knew the* Greyhound. *She was fast and had a great reputation for speed.*

"Well, we began to get ready for the run. I had the boys save the best of the fuel. We stowed in plenty of bark to fill up the holes in the firebox. Bark makes a terrific heat.

"The time of the race came and we went to it. I have forgotten who was engineer on the 'Hound' or who was our skipper. The Aberdeen hit it up at a good clip. When the boys passed the word back that the Greyhound's *crew were heaving their cordwood overboard I knew we had them. We beat them into the dock at Tacoma by some distance—in fact, when we docked the 'Hound' was nearer Browns point than the dock."*

Her racing days over, the *City of Aberdeen*

TODAY, AS THE ERIK FOSS, the former **Gleaner** and **ST-216** is a striking example of how old steamboats become sleek, modern diesel tugs. Captain James Henshaw and Engineer Godfrey Anderson took the **Erik** out in the summer of 1954 to join the **Foss 18** and **Sandra Foss** for ship handling and other harbor duties in the port of Seattle. Equipped with a 900-horsepower engine, mechanical steering gear and oversize rudder, the rejuvenated tug packs plenty of authority.

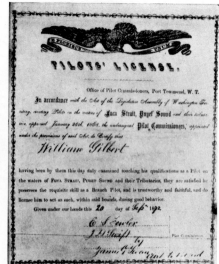

STEAM TUG JOHN CUDAHY, built at Ballard in 1900, teamed up with the steam tug **Gleaner** on war time towing missions. The two old-timers are still on the same team, and it's hard to decide which one has changed the most. The 57-year old **John Cudahy** is now the **Henry Foss.**

was laid up on the Duwamish River near Seattle in 1908. Contemporary newspaper accounts said she was falling apart from neglect and that somebody had built a dock in front of her mooring so she couldn't get out even if she wanted to. That should have been the end of the old paddler, but she extricated herself somehow, moving up to Bellingham as the towboat *Vashon.* In this guise she lasted several more years, dragging logs down the Skagit River and across Bellingham Bay.

More of the Sound stern-wheelers waited for a spell of good weather and headed down the coast to take up river towing jobs on the Columbia and Willamette. The fast *State of Washington* was one of these. After running passengers and freight between Puget Sound and Hood Canal ports from 1889 until 1913, she moved south to earn her living as a towboat for the Shaver Transportation Company. In 1921 she was shoving an oil barge up the river near Astoria when a sudden boiler explosion reduced her to scrap iron and kindling wood in a split second.

Other out-of-work paddlers like the *Telegraph* and *Capital City* followed in her footsteps to find less sensational ends in junkyards when the new diesel towboats came to take their jobs on the river.

There are no stern-wheel towboats left on Puget Sound or British Columbia waters now. One of the last of them was the *Swinomish*. Until a few years ago she was a colorful sight, puttering around Everett harbor or chuffing under the Snohomish River bridges.

On one occasion the little *Swinomish* was detailed to transfer a scowload of lumber from one of the Everett mills to a British ship moored in the harbor. The captain and mate of the limejuicer had never seen anything quite like the *Swinomish* and they watched her closely as she churned toward them.

As a unit of the American Tugboat fleet she was painted bright green and orange. Her tall, skinny smokestack emitted a cloud of black

THE AUDREY WAS LAUNCHED at Tacoma in 1909 as a 64-foot passenger and freight steamer. Changing with the times, she's now a diesel-powered towboat, a unit of Delta V. Smyth's Olympia towing fleet.

smoke, steam hissed from her 'scape pipe, her water wheel splashed sedately astern. The barn door on her boiler deck was slid back to reveal the fireman at work on the boiler fires. Alongside was a tremendous pile of finished lumber.

As she drew alongside, the British mate turned to his skipper to observe incredulously, "Gor'blimey, sir, you just cahnt tell what these bloody yanks will do next. *I do believe they're bringing their sawmill out to the ship!*"

LITTLE STEAM TUG ALICE, built at Alameda, California in 1892, probably wasn't designed as a racer, but like many of the West Coast's rejuvenated old-timers of the towing fleet, she's capable of kicking up her heels nowadays. As the **Foss No. 18** she has been a frequent winner in Seattle's Maritime Day Tugboat Races. The photo on the left shows the **Alice** as a plodding youngster. On the right, as the **Foss No. 18** she's shown digging in hard for the final sprint of the 1950 Seattle races.

DREDGES, AS WELL AS TUGBOATS, have changed their appearance and their power plants the past half century. Above, the steam dredge **San Diego,** tended by the little tug **Mayflower** scoops mud from Seattle's Duwamish Waterway to help form the city's industrial district. Note the barge of coal alongside to feed the **San Diego's** boiler fires.

Below, the Puget Sound Bridge and Dredging Company's powerful diesel **H. W. McCurdy** moves off in the wake of the **Hercules.** The fir tree at the **McCurdy's** masthead indicates that the picture was taken during the Christmas season.

STEWART C. OSBORN of Port Orchard, Washington wrote for **Pacific Motorboat** magazine for many years under the pen name "Scuttlebutt Pete". Although terribly crippled by arthritis, "Old Scut" knew the Northwest workboat fleet and the men who operate it because the tugboat men were his friends. He couldn't go to them, so they brought the news to him. He wrote it up in a salty, sunny style that was all his own. A few years ago the tugboat men threw a party for Scut. They brought him a short-wave radio and after that he got his news hot off the airwaves, listening to the news and gossip of the "tugboat band".

In April, 1954, **Pacific Motorboat** reported, "Aye lads, Ol' Scut passed on a bit of a tide ago". That's the way Stewart Osborn would have written it. He was mourned by tugboat men from Cape Blanco to Nome.

H. C. JAMISON (left) was another writer of West Coast towboat sagas. As one tugboat man said, "There are so many marine writers that don't know what they're talking about that you appreciate somebody like Jamison when he comes along". Jim Cary (right) is another waterfronter who is well versed in tugboat lore.

RIVER OF THE WEST

The stern-wheeler reached its highest development on the Columbia because the river was, until recent years, a waterway where stern-wheelers worked better than any other device for making steamboats go. Below Vancouver, the river has always been broad and comparatively placid. Screw and side-wheel steamers worked well enough there, but further east, as it was compressed by the sheer, rock walls of the Cascade Mountains' foothills, the river was narrow, the channel narrow and tortuous, the current swift. It was a white water river, and stern-wheelers are best for white water running.

The great wheel aft—close to the rudders—gave tremendous leverage for maneuvering the long, slim, shallow hull in swift water. Monkey rudders, placed aft of the wheel, bit into the wake churned up by the paddle-buckets to give added authority to the pilot's touch. The stern-wheel design had definite advantages over the side-wheeler in riverbank landings, too, whether scheduled, unexpected or purely accidental.

A stern-wheeler could nose into the bank to pick up passengers or freight in a nonchalant manner, secure in the knowledge that her wheel, back aft, could easily be kept in deep water. Side-wheelers like the *T. J. Potter* and the *Oneonta* sometimes ran into trouble when they tried this maneuver, for the current had a tendency to push one wheel into the shore, where it might get stuck in the mud. When this happened, stern-wheel pilots were accustomed to snicker unsympathetically while the atmosphere turned blue above the side-wheeler's pilot house. The stern-wheelers had another advantage, which may sound highly imaginative but is vouched for by old time steamboat men. In navigating some of the more shallow and wildly twisting tributaries of the big river, steamboat pilots travelled in reverse. They went up and down the streams backward, the wheel pulling instead of pushing the boat. They apparently went on the theory that if the wheel made the sharp turns the boat had to follow it, one way or another. Whatever the reasoning, the method worked and a number of minor streams were made navigable by stern-wheelers travelling in this unorthodox fashion. It was a sight that would probably have induced hysteria in any right-minded Mississippi River steamboat pilot, but it was only one of a number of Columbia River trade secrets calculated to have that affect on steamboat men used to the sluggish movement of the Big Muddy.

Like the time in 1881 when the big stern-wheeler *R. R. Thompson* went through the Cascades of the Columbia *at just under 60 miles an hour!* (She was timed through the narrow, twisting six-mile rapids at six minutes, 40 seconds). The *Mountain Queen* c a m e tearing through later the same year, and although her time was a bit slower she still ran away from an excursion train that had come down the shoreside track to watch the excitement. When the *Hassalo* made the run in 1888 the water was lower, which meant the channel was even narrower and more rocky fangs were sticking out to gore a passing steamboat, but she made it in just a few seconds over the *Thompson's* record time.

A number of upper Columbia stern-wheelers even plunged over the falls at Celilo, which is a little hard to believe if you've seen them . . .

PUSHING AN EMPTY BARGE ahead in proper river towboat style, the stern-wheeler **Rustler** passes lines of high-riding grain ships in Portland harbor as she prepares to dodge a down-river packet and a cross-river ferry on the busy Willamette.

or watched motion pictures of the Yakima Indians dipping salmon against a background of the white, raging cataract. The *Harvest Queen* made it, however, and so did the big *Umatilla* as well as ten or a dozen other venturesome stern-wheelers. Such voyages weren't standard practice, the boats making them only when economic necessity required that they be moved from one section to another. Normally there were lower river and mid-river and upper river boats. Passengers and freight were portaged by mule or steam powered railway from one boat to another until government locks were built to skirt the worst of the falls and rapids.

Even so, the boats on the mid and upper river runs bucked plenty of white water, and as long as that was the case stern-wheels were hard to beat. It was only when the face of the river was changed by a new trend in government construction that a new type of river boat came to take over the work of the pic-

turesque steamboats. The new development is the construction of huge dams to harness the tremendous hydro-electric potential of the Columbia. The dams aren't bars to navigation, for they are equipped with locks which lift ships quickly and safely to the level of the water behind them. But they are rapidly ironing out and obliterating the rushing, stone-fanged rapids and the falls which gave stern-wheelers their advantage over other types of river boats.

When Bonneville Dam, with its 500-foot ship lock, was completed in 1938 its imprisoned waters rose slowly to stifle the age-old roar of the Cascades. A placid lake now covers the rapids w h e r e the stern-wheelers boomed through at a mile a minute. It covers, too, the crumbling masonry of the Cascade Locks, built in later years to enable steamboats to detour around the worst of the rapids.

Now the rising waters of McNary Dam are making another quiet lake of the once brawling river as far inland as Pasco. Even the mighty

falls at Celilo are being blotted out and, while there are no steamboats left to go over them, salmon still work upstream, and the Yakima Indians are most unhappy at the steady disappearance of their tribal fishing grounds.

The first of the new boats designed to take full advantage of the Columbia's new look was really an old timer in new outfit, but she set a trend that has become almost universal, not only on the Columbia, but on all the inland waterway systems of America.

The *Shaver* started out in life as a typical river stern-wheeler in 1908, built for the Shaver Transportation Company. She operated in that role for some 18 years, but in 1926 she paddled over to the plant of the Willamette Iron and Steel Company to become the guinea pig in an experiment. Her stern-wheel was

amputated, her stern rebuilt in an unusual manner. Her tall, red-banded stack with its triple-chime steam whistle was replaced by a stubby funnel to vent the fumes from the two 400 horsepower diesels that went on the bed of the old steam engine.

Shortly thereafter the *Shaver* emerged as the first tunnel-stern twin-screw diesel towboat in America. From forward she didn't seem much changed. She still looked like a stern-wheel steamboat with her low hull and high stacked cabins, texas and pilot house. She even kept her king post and hog chains, so it was only when she swung broadside that it became evident something was missing. And, of course, there was no mistaking the thump and rumble of her diesels for the soft snoring of a steam plant . . . or the honk of her air horn for the

lonesome melody of steamboat's chime.

But the *Shaver* had made history with only minor changes in her appearance. Since her transformation thousands of river towboats have been built to the same basic pattern. Since they were built from scratch, they bear no resemblance at all to the old stern-wheel towboats. Most of them are fat and squatty with vestigual twin funnels squatting below the level of the pilot house, but their diesel engines, shallow hulls, and multiple screws set in tunnels aft are patterned on the old *Shaver*.

From a historical standpoint the *Western*, ex-*Shaver* does more than illustrate the transition in river towboats from paddle steamer to diesel screw. She's living evidence of the sort of mechanical immortality that is peculiar to inland steamboats. It's seldom that such a boat

ON A CALM DAY on the Columbia River bar one tug could sometimes bring in two or three sailing vessels on a single haul . . . in this case the barks **Portland** and **Tidal Wave** and the barkentine **Wm. Griffith.** Things aren't always that tranquil on the bar, however.

dies completely, unless she's destroyed by accident. A junked boat usually has most of her useable parts grafted onto newer craft to continue a useful life.

The 28 year old diesels of the *Western* rest in the engine bed and hull of the 1908-model stern-wheeler steamer *Shaver.* Her steam engines, removed in 1926, came from a 19th century steamboat called the *Hanford,* used to haul construction material for the first railway down the Washington shore of the river. A builder's plate on one of the engine's five-sided cast iron steam pipes indicated that it had been built by a Cincinnati, Ohio, firm in 1859! Further research revealed that the ancient *Hanford's* engines came originally from a packet named *Arkansas Chief* which operated on the Mississippi River system and served as a Union gunboat during the Civil War blockade.

Since the converted stern-wheeler showed the way to added efficiency and lower costs, many newer and some more powerful diesel towboats have joined the river fleet. The huge

Inland Chief, nearly 200 feet long, until she was cut down, could carry 850 tons of cargo in her hold in addition to the big steel barges she pushes up and down the river; more than was ever moved by the graceful white stern-wheelers of the steamboat era. More than two million tons of cargo are moved each year by barge and towboat. It's done with greater efficiency and with a mere handful of boats compared to the old fleet of paddlers.

Of course progress always brings nostalgia in its wake, and there are many who feel that the diesel towboats and their steel barges are poor substitutes for the stern-wheel steamboats. A string of barges shepherded through concrete locks by a snorting diesel is hardly a sight to be compared to a tall white steamboat coming down the rapids like an express train under a plume of wood smoke. The sad, sweet echo of steamboat whistles around the bend is gone from the middle and upper river, nor does the occasional hoot of a diesel horn adequately replace that traditional music.

WITH THUNDERING PADDLE-BUCKETS the towboat **Hercules** shoulders the barge **Washougal** up the Columbia River from Astoria toward Portland.

On the lower river and on the Willamette around Portland the new-fangled diesel propellers don't have it quite all their own way yet, however. There's the indestructible old *Henderson* wearing the red stack band of the Shaver Transportation Company, and there's Western Transportation Company's modern, semi-streamlined stern-wheel steamer *Jean*, which isn't quite in the classic tradition, but is an authentic steam-driven paddler just the same.

The steel-hulled *Jean* was built in 1938 and she's a compromise between classic river boat design and modern towboat construction. Her pile of houses—four stories from guards to pilot house—topping her low, shallow hull is traditional stern-wheel steamboat. But the deckhouses, as well as the hull, are of steel instead of wood; her superstructure is curved instead of angular as in the old boats. Instead of a single tall stack the *Jean* has a pair of short ones mounted side by side abaft the pilot house. Her stern-wheel, housed in a neat guard, looks much like those attached to the old timers, but it's really one of her major departures from tradition.

The *Jean's* wheel is really two wheels, mounted side by side under the same guard. Each half is separately powered and controlled, a device which makes her remarkably maneu-verable. With half the wheel turning ahead, the other half astern, and the rudders hard over, she can make sharp and sudden turns that would induce dizziness in an old time steamboat man. She can even travel sideways, in the manner of a crab, whenever the occasion arises. All in all, *Jean* is quite a boat.

So is the big steel stern-wheeler *Portland*, owned by the Port of Portland and operated by the Shaver Company. She replaced an older, wooden *Portland*, built in 1919 and retired in 1947. When the first tentative plans were made for her construction it was proposed to build the new *Portland* as a typical modern diesel towboat with tunnel stern and multiple screws and rudders. When the Willamette pilots, who would have to operate her, heard this heresy their protests and lamentations were long, loud, and effective enough to get the plans changed. The Willamette at Portland is narrow, full of tricky currents and often beset by gusty and unpredictable winds. The pilots felt nothing could beat a big stern-wheel steamboat for maneuvering ships in such waters, and it was conceded that they should know.

The paddle fleet has dwindled almost to the point of no return now. The *Georgie Burton* made her last trip up the river the year the new *Portland* was launched. People stood along the river banks all the way to watch her, for

PORT OF PORTLAND'S handsome stern-wheel towboat **Portland** looks like an old-timer, but is comparatively new. Steel-hulled and thoroughly modern in her equipment and fittings, she was launched in 1947.

FUSSING AND FUMING, a pair of Shaver stern-wheelers work a deep-sea log raft downstream on the Columbia.

she was the last stern-wheeler on the middle river and she wasn't coming back. Her owners, Western Transportation Company, had presented the old towboat to The Dalles and that once roaring river port had arrangements made to move her ashore to become a steamboat museum and a monument to the past. Unfortunately she wasn't moved far enough inland; the river took her back during the great floods of the following year. The dependable old *Georgie*, like almost all the other paddlers, is just a memory now.

Another famous Western boat, the 160-foot *Claire*, made her last voyage a couple of years ago when she made her annual pilgrimage to Champoeg with a crew of old time steamboat men. She's still intact at her moorings, but she won't be turning her wheel again. The river veterans make their annual journey now . . . and it's a painful thing to say . . . by bus.

So the *Portland* and the *Henderson* and the *Jean* are all that are left of an era. The *Portland* and *Jean* are made of steel, and steel ships, for some reason, never arouse the intimate affection that men feel for wooden ships. So the old *Henderson*[1] remains the sentimental favorite of Portland, a city which has a greater tendency than most Northwest cities to brood over the simple virtues of the past. Everyone was happy when the *Henderson* nosed out the big new *Portland* in a recent steamboat race on the Willamette. And the mere fact that there are still enough stern-wheel steamboats left to stage a race is comforting to those who are convinced a river needs a few towboats that are picturesque instead of merely utilitarian.

RIVER LINES

Many of the Pacific Northwest towing companies, like the boats they operate, have been around for a long time. At about the time the Foss Company was building its future around a few second-hand rowboats on Puget Sound, the Shaver Transportation Company was getting started on the Columbia River. This firm, which still operates most of the remaining Columbia stern-wheelers (the *Henderson* and the *Portland*), started operations with a single steamboat of that classic design, the *Manzanillo*.

Captain George M. Shaver, later president of the company, was master of the *Manzanillo* when she was commissioned as a brand new packet of the Peoples Freighting Company in 1884. He'd started out as a deckhand on Wil-

lamette River boats two years before, so he wasn't doing badly at all.

But Captain Shaver had more ambitious plans than running a steamboat for somebody else. He wanted a boat of his own, and he was partial to the *Manzanillo*. Before long the handsome stern-wheeler was earning profits for the newly-incorporated Shaver Transportation Company, which consisted of Captain George and his three brothers, James, Delmar and Lincoln.

The pioneer *Manzanillo*, under Captain Shaver's guidance, did so well that it wasn't long until plans were made for a new, faster boat, the *George W. Shaver*. The new steamer, named after the father of the four Shaver brothers, earned further profits, which went into a third boat.

This newest steamer was to be entered in the highly competitive Portland-Astoria trade, which meant that she had to be well above average in speed, comfort and good looks. The *Sarah Dixon* was all of that. She carried the name of the Shaver brothers' mother, an Oregon girl who met and married George W. Shaver when he arrived in the territory after the California gold rush, and she was a steamboat to be proud of. Not only was she fast and handsome; she was the most up-to-date boat on the river. She had a steam steering gear, the latest cargo loading machinery, and even the new-fangled luxury of electric lights.

The *Sarah Dixon's* first master was Captain George Shaver, with the famed river boat engineer "Poppy" Pope handling her smoothly powerful twin engines. Later Captain Fred G. Lewis took her over. Every old steamboat man has a favorite boat, it seems. One that hasn't been robbed of her speed and grace and beauty by the mist of time. Captain Lewis, going-on 90 now, has forgotten the names of a lot of steamboats he once knew, but he remembers the *Sarah Dixon*. "She was a sweet boat, was the *Sarah Dixon*; a mighty sweet boat," Captain Lewis will tell you.

As the fast new boats with the red bands on their smokestacks were added to the Shaver fleet, the old established steamboat operators were disturbed. The Red Collar boats seemed to be getting more than their share of the passenger and freight business, and something had to be done about it. Since they didn't seem to be frightened by threats of rate-cutting, the big companies were forced to play their trump card. They agreed to pay a subsidy to certain troublesome Shaver steamboats if their owners

1. As Pacific Tugboats went to press, word came from Portland that the Henderson, damaged in a collision with a freighter, has lost her Coast Guard certification and will be decommissioned. The old-timers are going fast.

LAST OF WESTERN'S OLD-TIME STERN-WHEELERS, the **Claire** is shown in action on the Willamette River near Salem in this 1944 photograph, taken by Western Transportation Company's president, L. M. Thompson. Now supplanted by modern diesel towboats, the **Claire** is still afloat at the Western moorings in Portland. (Photo courtesy of L. M. Thompson)

would keep them out of the freight and passenger trade.

Some of the boats thus b a r r e d from their usual line of work were used to perform towing jobs. This proved profitable, bringing about a gradual transition f r o m old - fashioned steamboating to a modern towing operation. The Shaver boats still carry the traditional red funnel band, but it has been years since any of them raced the White Collar or Yellow Stack boats to corral the freight and passenger business.

Captain George Shaver's son, Captain Homer T. Shaver, is present secretary-manager of the company which, in addition to the two picturesque stern-wheelers, operates a fleet of 23 diesel propeller tugs. Captain Homer Shaver's title isn't an honorary one. He learned his trade the hard way—on the river. As a small boy he spent summers and holidays running lines on the decks of the stern-wheelers. In later years he qualified as master and pilot of river boats.

Another big river t o w i n g firm, Western

Transportation Company, has finally tied up its last stern-wheeler, the *Claire*. Before she went out of commission the *Claire* kept an era alive, for she was the last paddle steamboat to operate on the upper Willamette. True, in her later years her voyages there were infrequent; once a year she took the Veteran Steamboat Men's Association to their meeting at Champoeg State Park on the river above Oregon City. Once in a while she paddled clear up to Salem to dredge out the mill pond with her stern-wheel.

Declared unfit for further service, she was tied up at the Western moorings on the Portland waterfront after she took the old timers on their last steamboat ride up the Willamette in 1952. Small diesel tugs still work the upper reaches of the river, but none of the remaining stern-wheelers are slim enough to negotiate the locks. The veteran river men have bowed to p r o g r e s s. They go to Champoeg by motor busses, and a steamboat whistle will never again echo off the mouth of the Yamhill or the Santiam.

THE OLD AND THE NEW. Above, a powerful diesel towboat of Tidewater-Shaver Barge Lines pushes an ammonia barge through the McNary Dam locks where the fury of Umatilla Rapids once blocked river navigation. With the smoothing out of the rapids by dams like this, the advantages of the stern-wheeler with its light draft and easy handling in white water no longer equalled the efficiency and economy of the diesel-driven propeller. Below, the stern-wheeler **Claire** is shown moving a barge on the lower Columbia in classic riverboat style. (Upper photo by Walla Walla District Corps of Engineers).

UNIQUE ON AMERICAN RIVERS is Western Transportation Company's steel stern-wheel steamer **Jean,** built in 1938 and equipped with ultra-modern gear for cargo handling and communications. Said to be the only boat of her type in the world, the **Jean** has two stern-wheels, each independently driven by two engines. The wheels can turn in opposite directions, enabling the **Jean** to make sharp turns, spin like a top, or even travel sideways like a crab. Designed by W. D. McLaren, Vancouver, B.C., who also designed the Canadian Pacific Empress liners, the **Jean** is one of the Columbia's three remaining stern-wheelers. In recent years the **Jean** has been in charge of such veterans as Capt. Amel Cejka, Engineers Orval Conaway, Harry Colson and Herbert L. Dotson and Pilot Edwin O. Mawhinney. The average Western Transportation Company service of these five men is 35 years. (Photo by Chester A. MacNeill, Jr.)

SKOOKUM SHIPS are Western's powerful sisters **George Birnie** and **Peter W.** Packing 3600-horsepower in their shallow hulls, these big riverboats are among the West's mightiest towing craft. Below, the **George Birnie** is shown moving under the Interstate Highway Bridge between Portland, Oregon and Vancouver, Washington. Not seen in the picture is the **Birnie's** record tow of four hemlock bundle rafts totaling 1,553,660 board feet. Above, the **Peter W.** tows five government YTM-class tugs under the St. Johns Highway Bridge . . . as the Portland **Oregonian** said, "Like a mother duck with her ducklings". (Photos by Chester A. MacNeill, Jr.)

UPPER COLUMBIA RIVER TOWING COMPANY'S powerful diesel towboat **Bannock** moves a loaded barge downstream through the McNary Lock. The barge, a type common to the Columbia River, is equipped to carry petroleum products upstream, bulk grain on the return voyage. (Walla Walla District Corps of Engineers Photo).

FAR FROM THE SEA, at Port Kelley in the sagebrush country of the upper Columbia River, the pusher-boat **Patricia** waits to move a grain barge downstream when it is fully loaded. It won't take long, since the Port Kelley elevators load cargo at the rate of 10,000 bushels per hour. (Photo by Walla Walla District Corps of Engineers).

TIDEWATER SHAVER'S MARY GAIL II shoves a loaded petroleum barge through the upstream lock and under the bascule bridge at McNary Dam. Sixty thousand tons of freight will pass through these locks in an average month. Above the dam is an amazing man-made lake, 292 miles long and more than 300 feet deep, providing slack-water navigation where dust was once raised by settlers' covered wagons. (Walla Walla District Corps of Engineers Photo).

TWILIGHT ON THE RIVER. (Opposite) Clouds of black smoke and the gilded wake of paddle-wheels paint a sunset picture on the Snohomish River as the stern-wheel towboats **T. C. Reed, Harbor Belle** and **Forrester** work a huge log boom downstream toward the Everett sawmills.

INLAND NAVIGATION COMPANY'S INLAND CHIEF, shown here being lifted to reservoir level at McNary Dam with the barge **Port of The Dalles,** was one of the first craft built especially for upper river navigation through the locks constructed by the U. S. Corps of Engineers. Built at Seattle in 1937, she was originally 190 feet long and able to stow 850 tons of cargo in addition to her tow. More recently she has been cut in two. The after section, with its 1200-horsepower diesels remains a towboat.

GRAYS HARBOR FERRY. In days long gone, the little tug **Thistle** and a barge provided ferry service across the Chehalis River at Aberdeen for horses and humans. There were no automobiles to complicate things.

GRAYS HARBOR

The Port of Grays Harbor, which includes the ocean-side fishing port of Westport and the river lumber ports of Aberdeen, Hoquiam and Cosmopolis, is the only haven, aside from Willapa Harbor, for ocean and coastwise shipping on the long run from the Columbia River to Puget Sound. The long stone jetties which mark its seaward limit have made Grays Harbor a safe and sheltered waterway, although when the winter storms sweep in from the Pacific the bar itself can be dangerous.

In more colorful days the major Grays Harbor ports of Aberdeen and Hoquiam were known far and wide as "tough towns," with scores of saloons built conveniently on piling above the Chehalis River. Celebrating sailors and loggers were frequently dropped through convenient trap-doors, either to be carried out to sea by the river or by the boats of crimps who delivered them, for a fee, to crew-hungry windjammers waiting on the lower bay.

Shortly after the turn of the century a greedy little man named Billy Gohl brought added notoriety to Grays Harbor. The local Seamen's Union secretary, Gohl won the confidence of working men by his determined and sometimes violent action against ship owners and mill operators in the labor battles of that era. Many of the sailors and loggers took to leaving part of their money with Billy Gohl before setting out for the perilous pleasures of the Grays Harbor skidroad.

Sometimes Billy's depositors took the trap-door route to oblivion and since few working stiffs of that day had families to worry about them, Billy kept their money. Soon he took to helping things along a bit himself by stalking his customers and knocking them over the head at opportune moments.

After a while Gohl's murder-for-profit business became so lucrative that he bought a small gas tug and a scow for carrying his corpses out to sea for burial. Still later he became lazy as well as greedy. Instead of towing the bodies of his victims out to sea, Billy Gohl began dumping them carelessly along the river bank. In the summer of 1910 more than forty bodies were dragged from the Chehalis River. Gohl was caught, imprisoned for life and died recently in a ward for the criminally insane.

There is as little monotony in present day Grays Harbor tugboating as there was in the colorful history of that region's past. Tugs based at Aberdeen and Hoquiam may be called upon to move logs down the twisting reaches of the upper Chehalis from the booming grounds near Montesano to the mills at Aberdeen or Hoquiam, or they may go plunging seaward in the teeth of North Pacific storms to assist some deepwater ship in trouble off the bar.

Two major tugboat companies serve the

Grays Harbor area, their operations extending from Montesano on the upper river to the bar, and sometimes well out to sea.

The Allman-Hubble Tug Boat Company of Hoquiam, with Captain F. P. Hubble as president and J. Neil Logue as manager, operates a fleet of six tugs for ship handling, general harbor towing and log towing in the harbor area. It has been in operation on the Harbor since 1909.

At Aberdeen the R. J. Ultican Tug Boat Company, headed by R. J. Ultican, Jr., is another pioneer firm which is active in the towing industry, with a fleet of well equipped diesel vessels and barges in regular service.

Grays Harbor is no longer the rip-roarin' seaport that it was in the days of Billy Gohl, but it still ships lots of lumber to the ports of the world, and Grays Harbor tugboat men are still tough and alert.

When the big Liberian freighter *Seagate* grounded on a reef north of Grays Harbor in September, 1956, mighty salvage tugs from Puget Sound and British Columbia sped down to see what they could do. But when the *Seagate* unexpectedly left her rocky perch in the face of an incoming storm she took them all by surprise. None of them had lines aboard when

THE SAUSE TUG, CHAHUNTA, is pictured at anchor inside the jetties at Westport after bringing a bargeload of logs safely through a winter storm which damaged other shipping along the coast.

THE SAUSE OCEAN TOWING COMPANY'S KLIHYAM takes green seas aboard as she crosses the Grays Harbor bar in the teeth of winter seas.

ALLMAN-HUBBLE'S 46-foot **Deck Boy** was built at Astoria, Oregon in 1928, is typical of the hard-working river tugs of Grays Harbor.

STERN - WHEEL TOWBOATS like Allman-Hubble's old **Harbor Queen** once worked the Chehalis River from Montesano to Aberdeen and Hoquiam. The **Harbor Queen,** an 86-footer, was built at Aberdeen in 1910. Here she's shown towing in typical stern-wheeler style, the tow line running through a block atop the king post.

she started her crewless cruise up the coast.

The big tugs started chasing her. The *Erik Foss* came racing out from Port Angeles. The *Island Sovereign* and *Island Commander* went slamming down from Canada. Other boats scurried about looking for the w a n d e r i n g freighter, but the little 500-horsepower Hoquiam harbor tug *A. G. Hubble* was the first to get a hawser and three men aboard the *Seagate* to establish salvage priority.

Which indicates that Grays Harbor tugs and tugboat men are pretty hard to beat in their own balliwick.

LOW FREEBOARD and high superstructure of the Allman-Hubble **Ranger** marked her as a typical river propeller tug. This is the way she looked in earlier days on the Chehalis River at Aberdeen and Hoquiam.

THE EPIC OF THE MAKEDONIA

Mac Reynolds, staff reporter of the Vancouver Sun, said, *"This is the story of a long tow, a dangerous tow and a fight to save a ship. For a month and more it has offered the world the most inspiring marine drama since the attempt of English tugs to rescue Capt. Kurt Carlsen's Flying Enterprise in the Atlantic, four years ago."*

"An incredible saga of brave men against the uncompromising sea," said Vancouver *Province* marine editor Norman Hacking.

NEW DIESEL-POWERED RANGER has replaced the old steamer on Grays Harbor waters. Here she's shown dragging a log boom past the old Harbor whaling station near Westport.

"*The most amazing salvage tow in history,*" was the way Ripley's *Believe It or Not* described it.

That was the epic of the Greek tramp freighter *Makedonia* and the British Columbia salvage tug *Sudbury*, flagship of the Island Tug and Barge fleet. It began on October 30, 1955, when the 8,200-ton *Makedonia*, six days out of Japan for Vancouver for a cargo of pyrites and lumber, broke down in mid-Pacific with a broken tail shaft.

Late the following day Island Tug and Barge dispatched the mighty steam tug *Sudbury*, a former Canadian Navy corvette, from Nootka to search out and bring in the helpless freighter, then 3,640 miles west of Vancouver and almost due south of the Kamchatka Peninsula of Siberia.

Caught in screaming gales and smashing seas, the *Makedonia*, with jury sails rigged fore and aft, wallowed westward at from 40 to 50 miles a day until the *Sudbury* reached her on the afternoon of November 12. Three hours later the *Makedonia* was under weigh, yawing rusty and highsided at the end of the *Sudbury's* 2000

BACK IN DECEMBER of 1947 the Allman-Hubble tug **Tyee,** based at Hoquiam, Washington, was engaged in towing logs down coast, Astoria to Tillamook Bay. On December 6 the **Tyee** had just completed a tow and was passing over the Tillamook Bar for the return voyage. The husky 78-footer crossed the bar, fighting through heavy seas, at 7:30 a.m. At 7:55 a huge sea carried away her steering gear and she immediately went out of control. Within minutes she was swept into the pounding surf, overwhelmed and sunk.

First reports indicated her entire crew of six had been drowned, but the Coast Guard Cutter **Onondaga** wirelessed the Bar View Coast Guard Station at 2:30 p.m. that she had picked up four men safely. The **Tyee** was later beached and found to be structurally sound. She was refloated, refitted and put back in service by the Foss Launch and Tug Company as the **Sandra Foss,** serving as a harbor tug at Seattle.

The pictures on this page show the saga of the **Tyee** from peaceful log towing on the Chehalis River to shipwreck on the ocean beach and eventual rejuvenation as the **Sandra Foss.**

THE SUDBURY (next two pages) shown towing the Greek freighter **Makedonia,** during the longest and probably the most difficult salvage tow in the history of the Pacific Coast—3,200 miles across the North Pacific in winter, with storms and gales reaching 80 m.p.h., over a period of 30 days—November - December, 1955.

feet of plow-steel towing cable. By November 16 tug and tow were fighting through hurricane-force gales and tremendous following seas that slowed their progress to a bare three knots.

Things were little improved next day, but the *Sudbury* found time for another good deed. Her radio operator, Percy Pike, picked up a faint distress call from an isolated Aleutian island called Sanak. A baby had been born there, there were complications, the mother was paralyzed and near death. For 24 hours the *Sudbury's* operator r e l a y e d medical information from government surgeons to Sanak until a U.S. Coast Guard plane evacuated the mother and her baby to a mainland hospital. Both survived and the baby was later christened Percy, in honor of the *Sudbury's* life-saving radio operator.

Arriving at Adak the next day, efforts were made to repair the *Makedonia's* damaged shaft so that she could proceed under her own steam. After two days the freighter was in shape to help out by turning her propeller at low speed, but it was decided that the *Sudbury* would have to complete the tow. On November 21 the *Sudbury's* master, Captain Harley Blagborne, reported that the ships were in the Bering Sea, the *Makedonia's* engines turning at half speed. The following day they were groping through a severe blizzard, working t o w a r d Unimak Pass. The weather cleared temporarily, but on November 24, south of Kodiak and heading into the Gulf of Alaska, tug and tow ran into a southeasterly gale w i t h winds eventually reaching 70 miles an hour.

In the midst of the storm the *Makedonia's*

RUGGED POWER RATHER THAN BEAUTY is inherent in the lines of a working tugboat's hull. Shown here in drydock as the United States Army Mineplanter **Armistead,** the **Agnes Foss** shows the hidden power that has given her the victory in epic battles with the sea.

S. S. **TRITON BEING TOWED** into Esquimalt Harbour, Victoria, B.C., by the **Lloyd B. Gore** after colliding with S.S. **Baranoff** off Gabriola Island in Strait of Georgia, July 26, 1952. Tug **Skookum** shown on right (below left). Patch fabricated on **Triton** to tow vessel to Esquimalt. Later was removed in drydock (right).—(Photos courtesy Island Tug and Barge, Ltd.)

propeller worked loose again and her engines shut down. Then the freighter's anchor chain, to which the *Sudbury's* tow line was made fast, parted. From the wildly pitching tug, the Canadian seamen watched the red and green lights of the helpless freighter blink out in the inky darkness, but they had other problems to occupy their minds. While Capt. Blagborne followed the drifting *Makedonia* on the radar screen, the crew struggled with snaking lines on the after deck waist-deep in smashing seas. Trailing behind them, threatening their propeller, was their long tow line and 30 tons of the *Makedonia's* anchor cable. Mate James Talbott was clipped on the head by a flip of the anchor chain, but there were no serious injuries and the lines were secured at last.

It was not until noon of the following day that the *Sudbury* again caught up with the *Makedonia,* and it took five nerve-wracking tries to get a line aboard. Then the big tug struggled back on course, heading south again. From then on there were gales and smashing seas all the way, but the *Sudbury* held on doggedly and her 2,750-horsepower quadruple-expansion steam engine never faltered. At 5:40 p.m., Sunday, December 11, the two ships passed under Lion's Gate Bridge, safe at last in Vancouver harbor. For the *Sudbury* it was the forty-second day of an ordeal seldom equalled in the annals of the sea.

MONKEY RUDDERS abaft the paddle buckets gave added maneuverability to Northwest river stern-wheelers. (Below left) Head of C. H. Cates and Sons is Capt. John Cates, eldest son of the firm's founder. (Below right) Capt. Grant Evans, well known Northwest towboat man.— (Cates photos courtesy Capt. C. W. Cates).

SAN FRANCISCO

San Francisco and Puget Sound tugboating have many similarities. In both areas, deep-sea and bay towing was the prerogative of deep-draft propellers and side-wheelers, with lanky, shallow-hulled stern-wheelers hauling loaded barges up the tributary rivers. Big stern-wheelers like the *San Joaquin No. 4*, built in 1885 as "the most powerful riverboat in America" (she had 478 h.p.), sometimes towed as many as five barges in tandem up the San Joaquin and Sacramento.

Then, too, many of the boats themselves had a habit of shuttling back and forth between the Golden Gate and Peter Puget's salty inland sea. It was a trend that started with ancient side-wheelers like the *Cyrus Walker* and *Goliah* (1), and has continued to this day. Almost as well known in one region as in the other are such names as *Bahada, Humacona, Vigilant, Alice, Katy, Sea King, Rabonni, Iroquois* and a score of others.

On San Francisco Bay, too, just as on Puget Sound, much of the work of harbor tugs was, in early days, done by open skiffs with a pair or two of stout arms at the oars. The "Whitehall" boats of San Francisco Bay specialized in carrying men and supplies to arriving and departing ships and in the process they would go almost anywhere. The 30-mile row from the Embarcadero to the Farallones was all in the day's work.

The power-plant of one of these early day harbor tugs was Tom Crowley, who entered the business of moving people and cargo on the bay at the age of 15, well before the turn of the century.

Tom Crowley's oar-powered Whitehall boat eventually developed into the Crowley Launch and Tug Company, one of the three dominant towing firms on the bay in sailing ship days. The other two were the "Red Stack" tugs of the Shipowners' and Merchants' Towboat Company and the Spreckles Towboat Company. Many and bitter were the battles between the boats and men of these rival fleets for supremacy on San Francisco Bay.

When Johnny Hislop, the famous Point Lobos lookout, sighted an incoming sail on the horizon and notified the Merchant's Exchange, it was usually only a matter of minutes before two or more rival tugs would be ramping through the Golden Gate, racing to be first with a line aboard the inbound windjammer.

Frequent contestants in those days were Capt. McCoy of Red Stack's *Sea Queen* and Capt. Dan Thomsen of the Spreckles' *Vigilant* (later Puget Sound's third *Goliah*). The tale is told of one foggy morning when both tugs went hooting out toward the Farallones in the midst of a blinding tule fog, looking for a square-rigger reported off the islands. The fog became so thick that a temporary truce was declared. The two boats hove to in a convenient cove and the crews whiled away the time in the soothing sport of rock cod fishing.

Capt. Thomsen of the *Sea Queen* knew that the *Vigilant* was a faster boat and that he must rely on his wits to defeat her, so he quickly

171

BIG STEAM TUG DEFIANCE, having brought a square-rigger safe inside the Golden Gate, squares away in search of another job.

RED STACK TUG SEA PRINCE, a 75-foot steamer built at San Francisco in 1901, was sunk so suddenly that all hands except the captain were drowned.

hatched a plan. "Keep your lines close to the top, boys," he told his crew. To the engineer he said, "Burn coal and keep the steam high."

When the *Vigilant's* crew was deeply engrossed in deep-line fishing and her steam pressure had ebbed considerably, the *Sea Queen's* shallow lines came in with a rush, the gong clanged in the engine room and the tug went boiling away at full speed in the general direction of Point Reyes. It took a good twenty minutes of profane activity to get steam up on the *Vigilant* and head off in the supposed wake of the *Sea Queen.*

The wily Thomsen, however, had changed course for the Cordell Banks, where the fog was even thicker and the fishing better. By mid-afternoon the *Sea Queen's* deck was piled with fresh fish and the fog was clearing a bit. Soon the masts and spars of a square-rigger showed up through the shredding mist. It was the ship they had been looking for, almost on top of them.

After assuring himself that Capt. McCoy's *Vigilant* was nowhere in sight, Thomsen eased the *Sea Queen* over to dicker with the ship's master as to the towing fee. His figure was $600. The shipmaster held tough at $500, but

POWERFUL STEAM TUG FEARLESS, built by Union Iron Works in 1892, was designed for the Spreckles Towboat Service, but she spent most of her time serving the U. S. Government, during the Spanish-American War as the **Fearless**, in the two World Wars as the **Iroquois**.

Capt. Thomsen noticed that all hands aboard the windjammer were eyeing his fresh-caught fish hungrily. At the psychological moment he asserted that he couldn't possibly lower his price, but for $600 he would tow the ship to port and throw in his fine mess of fish.

The windship skipper grumbled loudly that it was the most expensive damn' mess of fish he'd ever bought, but he signed the book and took the *Sea Queen's* line and the tow was under way by the time the *Vigilant* came charging out of the vanishing fog with Capt. McCoy far gone in rage and frustration.

Such was San Francisco towboating at the turn of the century and the man who emerged at the top of the heap was Capt. Tom Crowley. Not only did his own firm, the Crowley Launch and Tug Company, grow and prosper, but the Crowley firm now controls the Red Stack tugs too. And the Spreckles Towboat Company is no more. Subsidiary companies of the Crowley towboat empire extend from Southern California to Puget Sound.

Of course San Francisco tugboating has its share of adventure too; some tragic, some just embarrassing, as when, in 1910, the launch

Crowley II, with Capt. Lindstrom at the wheel, ran aground on a defunct whale.

The *Crowley II* was easing along at eight knots through a pea soup fog when her motion suddenly ended in a horrible jar which caused the perplexed Capt. Lindstrom to bump his nose painfully on the pilot house window. His craft seemed to be aground, but he knew he was far out in the harbor with plenty of water under his keel. When he opened a pilot house window

VIGILANT, formerly the **George W. Pride, Jr.,** came to San Francisco in 1886 to work for the Spreckles Towboat Company. In later years she served on Puget Sound as the **Goliah** (2).

CROWLEY NO. 28 was built at Alameda in 1927 as a harbor workboat for the Crowley Launch and Tugboat Company. Like most tugs built after 1925, she was powered with a diesel engine. The 80-foot Crowley No. 28 is now the Tyee, working at Seattle for the Puget Sound Tug and Barge Company.

for a better look forward the mystery was explained. The explanation hit him in the form of an overpowering stench from the rammed whale which, long dead, had floated unseen through the Golden Gate. The launch had rammed her way deep into the rotten carcass and was so well stuck that it seemed the crew might be overcome by the awful smell before they were released.

At length, however, by dint of much pike pole pushing and violent reversal of the engine, the *Crowley II* won free. Her crew claimed that she didn't smell just right for six months afterward, however.

Then there was the Red Stack tug *Sea Prince*, sunk so suddenly that only the captain escaped. Piloting the British tramp *Greystoke Castle* down from Port Costa, the *Sea Prince* was eas-

SEA QUEEN, a Red Stack 100-footer, built at San Francisco in 1888, specialized in the highly competitive business of towing inbound windjammers from the Farallones to San Francisco Bay. For many years she was skippered by Capt. Dan Thomsen, who later towed the Goliah around the Horn with the Hercules.

SEA LARK WAS TYPICAL of the smaller San Francisco Bay tugs of the Red Stack company in days of sail and steam. Built at San Francisco in 1905, the 78-foot **Sea Lark** developed 250-horsepower with her compound steam engine. She carried a four man crew, about the minimum for a steam vessel.

ing down the bay with Capt. Langren at the wheel. The rest of the crew was at dinner in the galley when something went wrong. Capt. Langren, feeling the loom of a shadow which seemed to blot out the sun, looked over his shoulder to see the great bow of the freighter hanging like a mountain over the little tug's stern. Even as he gave the signal for full speed ahead and opened his mouth to shout a warning to his crew, the massive prow cut through the tug's steel hull like a giant knife through a wedge of cheese.

Seconds later the *Sea Prince* was trampled under by the vast weight of the oncoming ship. Lifeboats, hurriedly lowered after the crash, found only bits of floating wreckage and the tug's skipper, who had been swept from the pilot house and left floating on the surface.

From Alaska to San Francisco Bay, the West Coast tugboats engage in rugged, man-sized jobs. It's only once in a great while that the odds prove too great for the little ships and the men who serve them.

TUG GOLDEN GATE, built originally as a Coast Guard rescue vessel for San Francisco, was the first major vessel built by the famous old Seattle shipyard of Robert Moran. Launched at high noon on Sunday, February 14, 1897, with a ceremony attended by two ex-governors, Seattle's mayor and city council and 5000 other spectators, the husky 110-foot steamer served Bay Area shipping for almost half a century.

TUGBOAT TALES

Pacific Northwest tugboat men are prone to shrug or laugh off any effort to picture their work as anything but another way to earn a living. For 364 days out of the year they play down the often dangerous, sometimes heroic, aspects of their trade. But during one day of the year a large number of them have been known to get together, let down their hair, and listen to each other's exploits. False modesty is, for the moment, thrown aside and the truth is sometimes badly fractured in the telling of the more colorful yarns.

They even hand out valuable prizes to those who give forth with the best—and the tallest—tales. All in all, it's quite an occasion, that one night of the year when the tugboaters get together to let off steam.

This informal association of workboat men in the Puget Sound region was the brain child of a yachtsman; a tugboat-admiring yachtsman named Jack Shipley. Aboard his cruiser, *Silver Spray,* Shipley whiled away many an idle hour listening to the radio's tugboat frequency, frequently alluded to as "the gossip band." It soon occurred to him that a great deal of fascinating folk-lore was being wasted on thin air. A lot of the weird and wonderful yarns he heard on the "gossip band" were, he felt, worth preserving.

So Shipley went on the air to propose a yarn-spinning contest, offering to put up a prime ham (he was in the meat distribution business) to the winner. His idea was taken up with such enthusiasm that it became an annual affair,

participated in by hundreds, and it led to the formation of that unique brotherhood of the tow line, the Puget Sound Piling Busters' Association.

As contributions to the first contest poured in from all over the Sound, the original plans were expanded considerably. Other yachtsmen who were "gossip band" fans wanted to put up prizes, too. Tugboat company owners weren't backward about contributing, either. By the time the Piling Busters assembled for drinks and dinner (paid for by the Tacoma Athletic Commission) there were 30 prizes on hand. Since the 50 yarns entered in the first contest were spun by a total of 35 tugboat men, practically everyone was a winner; a fine feature in any contest.

Mayor John Anderson of Tacoma put up an impressive gold cup for the winner in the Tall Tales division, the form of literary endeavor in which tugboaters shine the brightest. Competition was keen, but the grand prize went to Captain E. J. Stork of the *Simon Foss.* His highly plausible account of "The Time the *Simon Foss* Had Wheels" won the honor for him. Seems the *Simon* was trying to work a log boom out of Olympia's shallow East Waterway on a falling tide. It was a rush job, so Captain Stork was horrified when his boat grounded before he could get the logs lined up and out to deep water. Turned out fine, though, when he found that the under water obstruction on which his tug's hull was cradled was an old Ford chassis, complete with wheels.

THE ISKUM, NOW A UNIT of the Pioneer Towing Company fleet of Seattle is a frequent and spectacular participant in tow boat races. In other days she was operated by Capt. Lillicoe in Seattle harbor service. On one occasion, while carrying a load of fruit and vegetables to an anchored sailing ship, Capt. Lillicoe and the Iskum were attacked by a flock of hungry sea gulls. The Iskum's skipper was almost pecked into defeat by the piratical gulls, but he finally won the strange naval battle by turning live steam on the gulls, who retreated . . . carrying most of the Iskum's cargo with them.

DEFENDER ONCE WORKED as a harbor boat for Puget Sound Tug and Barge Company. The even smaller steamer Monohan (below) juggled logs on Lake Sammamish near Seattle.

Of course the *Simon Foss* had it made then. She just rolled over the muddy bottom on her rusty wheels, skidding a little on the sharp turns, but rounding up her logs in fine shape. Then she headed out toward deep water, rolling along smoothly until she reached a depth where wheels were no longer needed. Then she floated off to become an ordinary tugboat again.

It was quite a story, and there's no doubt that Captain Stork deserved his prize, but it wasn't quite as tall as most people seemed to think. Some 80 years ago a vessel did actually navigate that same muddy East Waterway in much the manner described in the Piling Busters' tallest of tall tales.

Back in the 1870's the Olympia - Shelton steamboat route was served, after a fashion, by a remarkable steam scow named *Capital*. This primitive craft was operated by a Captain Chapman and an alchoholic Squaxon known as Indian Vic. Upon one dramatic occasion Indian Vic allowed the *Capital's* boiler water to become depleted when the craft was still a couple of miles away from Olympia. As the boiler was beginning to jump up and down and bulge at the seams, both master and engineer thought it best to remove themselves from its range.

Captain Chapman followed Indian Vic overboard. Since they had been navigating close to shore, they were soon on the beach watch-

BIG STEAM TUG HUMACONA once hauled logs on Puget Sound for the Merrill and Ring Lumber Company. In recent years she transferred her operations to San Francisco Bay, where she moves car ferries for the Western Pacific Railway.

ENGINEER OTTO FREINER was handling the throttle on Northwest tugboats when this picture was taken. He is now an engineer on sea-going steamships in the trans-Pacific trade.

ing the *Capital* splash on toward Olympia between its two big side-wheels. They kept their hands over their ears and were prepared to duck, for they expected the whole works to explode at any moment.

But instead of exploding the *Capital* waddled right on down the East Waterway until she came to the expanse of bare mud exposed by the ebbtide. Even then she didn't so much as hesitate. She climbed right up on the mudflat and went slogging on toward town, rolling along on her paddle-wheels.

Captain and engineer watched open-mouthed as their versatile scow put on a preview of things to come. The *Capital* was the first amphibious landing craft! She kept right on rolling along on her big wheels until she fetched up against a piling, where she spun her wheels impotently until she ran out of steam.

She never did blow up, although Indian Vic took the pledge and left the sea for a mission school, while Captain Chapman never fully trusted her thereafter. Nobody took the hint she provided, the Army DUKW not putting in its amphibious appearance for another two generations.

And after 80 years her exploit was adapted to modern tugboat lore to win first prize for impossibility. If nothing else, the steam scow *Capital* proved that truth can be at least as

THE INTREPID, Bellingham Tug and Barge veteran, was one of the last steam tugs in service on Puget Sound. Built at Ballard in 1900, she was originally the **Charles Counselman.**

strange as fiction.

Captain Stork received his prize from Henry Foss, who didn't indicate that he was disturbed about one of his boats running around Olympia harbor on a set of Model-T wheels. The Piling Busters had elected him "Mr. Towboat" for 1951. Since Puget Sound maritime writers named C. Arthur Foss as Maritime Man of the Year 1951 this gave the Foss brothers a clean sweep on official marine honors that season.

Other major prize winners, who went home with such trophies as barometers, radios, electric clocks, cases of liquid cheer . . . and that original Shipley ham, were Harry Laviguer of the *Iver Foss*, John Cowan, *Favorite*, Captain Walter Torgesen, *Crosmor*, Captain David Livingston, *Arlyn Nelson*, W. O. Thaine, *Anne W.*, Elmer Edwards, *Carl Foss*, Walt Nelson, *Anne W.*, and Captain M. F. Galligan of the *Louise II*.

Captain Galligan was one of the first of the working boatmen to throw his whole-hearted support behind Shipley's original brainchild, has been a leading Piling Buster ever since. His tug, *Louise II*, has long been a colorful member of the Sound towing fleet. If the tug's bright green paint job isn't sufficient to indicate where Captain Galligan's loyalties lie, the large green shamrocks on each side of the pilot house are.

Captain Galligan always kept his tug handily moored off his Gig Harbor waterfront home,

CAPT. GUNNAR JOHNSON of the **Anne W.** and his brother, Capt. Otto Johnson of the **Tartar.**

THE SLEEK TIGER, fast and powerful flagship of the Cook Inlet Tug and Barge Company, was built in 1927 as a Coast Guard cutter. She has since been rebuilt and repowered to work the Anderson Brothers' Seattle-Anchorage run.

ALASKA TOWBOATING can be rugged work now as fifty years ago when the old **Resolute** sailed the northern sea lanes. In the photograph below, the **Resolute's** crew is shown chipping away at tons of ice on decks and houses while the cook bosses the job.

where it was easy to ship a crew. When a job came up, the *Louise II* usually put to sea with a full crew of Galligans, from captain to cook, and if the steaks were s c o r c h e d the cook couldn't count on hearing no more about it from the skipper when that voyage ended. With parental discipline added to the normal perquisites of a captain, the *Louise II* is handled in a smart and shipshape manner.

Under the guiding hands of Galligan and Shipley, the Puget Sound Piling Busters enjoyed a steady growth in popularity and membership. Most of the yarns submitted to the association's judges have been immortalized in various editions of the "Piling Busters' Yearbook," well-edited little books which are becoming real collectors' items. Browsing through a copy of the "Yearbook" is as entertaining as

FORMERLY OLSON TUG BOAT Company's Capt. **O. G. Olson,** the **Karen** now moves log booms between Wrangell and Ketchikan, Alaska for the Campbell Towing Company of Wrangell.

HAPPY PILING BUSTERS sample kettle of something or other. With them is Mrs. Hugh Gilmore, wife of one of Puget Sound's best known old-time tugboat captains. (Below) At 1953 Piling Busters' Banquet, "Mister Towboat" pennant for the past year is presented to Capt. James Dunlap, operator of the Dunlap Towing Company fleet on the Skagit River. Jack Shipley looks on from right, while Capt. Marion Galligan is still counting the crowd . . . a surprise turnout of 350 people.

eavesdropping on the "gossip band."

You'll chuckle over Vern Wright's account of the sea-going pig which boarded the *Iver Foss* in Hammersley Inlet, the trials and tribulations of the ubiquitous "green deck hand" searching for red and green oil to put in the running lights and sounding the water tank when the captain, afraid of grounding on a shoal, wanted to know how much water there was. Or the new cook on Art Torgesen's *Madrona* wondering why stumps were growing way out there when an Elliott Bay channel buoy was sighted. Or the one about the ambitious young crew member of the *Mary D. Hume* who was studying for his certificate of proficiency as mate of inland steam vessels. Seems his wife attended a party at which she mentioned her husband's activities.

Whereupon an interested, if somewhat confused, lady asked brightly, "My dear! Doesn't Frank have his mating license *yet?*"

As the Piling Busters' fame spread, its an-

TUGBOAT RACING IS A POPULAR SPORT in the Pacific Northwest, comparable to horse racing in Kentucky. In this 1949 race, the boats fought it out all the way from Seattle to Tacoma. It was almost dark when they entered Commencement Bay and Photographer Williamson snapped this dramatic scene, probably one of the finest tugboat racing pictures ever made. More recent races have been held on a shorter course in Elliott Bay.

nual meetings became more than just yarn-swapping sessions. In addition to the "Mr. Tugboat" award, which went to LeRoy Willey of the Olympia Towing Company at the second gathering, new forms of recognition were added. At the 1953 meeting, held in Seattle, Capt. James Dunlap was named Mr. Tugboat for the preceding year. His firm, the Dunlap Towing Company of LaConner, operates the largest fleet of river tugs in the Puget Sound region, specializing in towing logs down the tricky Skagit River to salt water.

The Norman Reilly Raine "Tugboat Annie

NORTHWEST WORKBOAT MEN take their racing seriously. Here the crew of the **Aleutian Native** is shown polishing their craft's bottom before entering her in a Seattle Maritime Day contest.

Oscar" was unveiled for the first time. This trophy, the gift of the author of the Saturday Evening Post Tugboat Annie stories, went to Piling Buster Warren Larson, Tacoma Tug and Barge Company. His tale of a winter-bound tow extricated with the aid of inflated doughnuts from the galley was well qualified to take its place with the other prize-winning whoppers in the Piling Buster archives.

It was at this gathering, too, that Capt. Noel Davis of the *Monarch* received the gold trophy and plaque of the Bardahl Oil Company's Workboat Service Trophy for the exploit which has been described in a previous chapter.

But the stories are the thing, and no book on tugboating would be complete without one Piling Buster yarn in its original and unexpurgated form. This one, by L. L. Riggs, Tacoma Tug and Barge dispatcher, concerns the gas tug *Dot*, a diminutive craft of some nine tons net register and slightly more than twice that much horsepower:

"It seems that one Johnny—operator of the tug Dot (all of 20 h.p.) working out of Rosedale—had delivered a tow of mining props to a ship in Seattle. This occurred late in June, when the tides up through the Narrows run like hell, so the Dot did not have the power to buck them. Johnny conveniently used this as an excuse for the crew off the Dot, captain and one deck hand, to go up town in Seattle in the neigh-

THE PHOENIX X, an ex-fish packer turned tugboat, moves the old Puget Sound steamer **Manitou** up Portage Bay toward a permanent mooring on the Seattle waterfront. The **Manitou** serves as a floating clubhouse for the Tyee Yacht Club.

STERN-WHEELER'S ENGINE ROOM is far different from that of a modern diesel towboat. The oil-fired boiler of the Army Engineer's workboat **W. T. Preston,** above, feeds steam to a pair of engines like the one shown below. Power is transmitted to the wheel by the long pitman-rods extending aft from the engine.

borhood of Yesler and make a few purchases. *The water on the Dot being bad, it was necessary to secure a few liquids to slake their thirst on the way home.*

Properly fortified for the long trip, Johnny and the Dot took off for Rosedale, but in the neighborhood of Shoreacres the tide was again wrong, so Johnny put in to the dock and made the Dot fast. The deck hand did the securing while Johnny made a little lunch to go with the beer.

Johnny awakened about low water, and preparatory to taking off down the Narrows with the fair tide, he went out on deck to look around, but it was so darned dark he could not see a damned thing, so Johnny took care of "nature" as the Dot had no plumbing. After relieving himself over the side as usual, Johnny noticed that it took one hell of a long time to hear a splash. Grabbing a lantern and lighting it, he tied it to a line and lowered it overside.

THE DOUGLAS WORKS THE OLD FOUR-MASTER LA MERCED, now a floating fish processing plant, through the open draw of the Ballard Bridge, en route to the Alaska fishing banks.

Sixteen feet to the water!

That damned deck hand had been too lazy to get lines long enough for slip lines, so had just "chokered" the piling. There they were, with the Dot *hanging up like a lifeboat in a set of davits.*

Johnny looked the situation over, called the erring deck hand and then, believe it or not, (Johnny says that it is true) he rigged a couple of lines to the top of the dock and carefully lowered the Dot *back into the waters of Puget Sound, all 36 feet of her; started up the engine and ran on down to Rosedale,—and up to now, this story has been kept a careful secret because Johnny didn't want his wife to hear it, as she might have doubted his veracity."*

There are poets among the Piling Busters, too. Sam Emmerson, Jr., of the Foss Tacoma fleet is responsible for this one:

> *"If for lack of influence*
> *You feel that life is dull*
> *A tug boat is the place for you*
> *You'll find that it has pull."*

And there's that bard of the pike pole, Tacoma Tug and Barge Company's A. N. (Scotty) Huntley, whose opus has been chosen for the last page so that domesticated tugboat men can, without damaging the rest of the book, tear it out and throw it away before their wives see it:

FOUR SEPARATE LOG BOOMS with their tugs can be seen in this unusual picture taken from the Deception Pass highway bridge.

"Come listen to our song, Lads,
Of men so brave and true;
We're hard and tough,
Ready and rough,
We're a gallant tugboat crew!

We'll take her out in any clime,
In wind or rain or shine;
At our daily work
We never shirk,
And we put her in on time.

We're welcome anywhere, Lads,
We're never out of hand;
We sing this song as we sail along
And we fear not any man.

We like our whiskey straight, Lads,
We like our rum and gin;
We tip the cup
Bottoms up,
Then fill 'em up again.

We get our lot of loving,
Wherever we may roam.
The girls, they sigh
As we draw nigh,
For us they'd leave their home.

So line up to the bar, Lads,
Tap that keg of brew;
Then hoist your beer
With a hearty cheer—
To a gallant tugboat crew!"

TUGBOATS ARE LIABLE to be called upon to move most anything. In this case it's a giant sawmill waste burner headed for the scrap yard with help from the **Martha Foss** and **Lorna Foss.** The **Martha Foss** has since been sunk in a collision with the Puget Sound steamer **Iroquois.** (Opposite) The famous Hawaiian Island schooner **Commodore** comes slashing in from a trans-Pacific voyage to take a line from the tug **Goliah.**

LADY COOKS are more frequently found on Columbia River towboats than on the tugs of Puget Sound, but Mrs. Meta Shaw, veteran galley boss of the Olson tugs **Madrona** and **Manzanita,** has been sailing the salt waterways of the Pacific Northwest since World War II days. She's a mighty fine cook, too. (Right) The junior deck hand of the **Manzanita** goes aloft. (Below left) A ready hand with pike pole and steady foot on a boomstick are prerequisites for successful tugboat men. (Below right) Puget Sound Maritime Historical Society "relic hunter" going after the whistle of the retired tug **Pioneer.**

PORT OF BANDON. Oregon's husky 80-footer, **Port of Bandon,** works a loaded steam schooner down the bay toward the Pacific. The **Port of Bandon,** built at Prosper, Oregon in 1938, is powered by a 500-horsepower diesel. (Below) The old **Olympic,** an 85-footer built at Ballard in 1900, picks up a boom of logs on Hood Canal. Capt. Ludlow, her skipper, is on the upper deck, mate Hugh Gilmore on the stern and cook Frank Scougale at the galley door. The men on the boom are not identified.

SELECTED BIBLIOGRAPHY

Andrews, Ralph W., *This Was Seafaring*, Seattle, 1955.

Bancroft, Hubert Howe, *History of Oregon*. 2 v. San Francisco, 1888.

—————————, *History of Washington, Idaho and Montana*, San Francisco, 1890

Binns, Archie, *The Roaring Land*, New York, 1942.

—————————, *Sea in the Forest*, New York, 1953.

Coman, Edwin T., Jr. & Gibbs, Helen M., *Tide Time and Timber*, Stanford, 1949.

Fitzsimmons, James, *Columbia River Chronicles*, British Columbia Historical Quarterly, I (1937).

Gaston, Joseph, *Portland, Oregon; its History and Builders*, Chicago and Portland, 1911.

Gibbs, James A., Jr., *Pacific Graveyard*, Portland, 1950.

Hanford, C. H., *Seattle and Environs*, v I, Chicago and Seattle, 1924.

Lamb, W. Kaye, *The Advent of the Beaver*, British Columbia Historical Quarterly, II (July, 1938).

MacMullen, Jerry, *Paddle-Wheel Days in California*, Stanford, 1944.

MacMullen, Jerry, and McNairn, Jack, *Ships of the Redwood Coast*, Stanford, 1945.

McCurdy, James G., *By Juan de Fuca's Strait*, Portland, 1937.

—————————, *Tugboats of the Northwest Coast*, Overland Monthly, 1908.

Merchant Vessels of the United States. Washington, D.C., 1868 - 1954.

Mills, Randall V., *A History of Transportation in the Pacific Northwest*, Oregon Historical Quarterly, XLVIII (September, 1946).

—————————, *Stern-Wheelers up Columbia*, Palo Alto, 1947.

Newell, Gordon R., *Ships of the Inland Sea*, Portland, 1951.

—————————, *S.O.S. North Pacific*, Portland, 1955.

Secretary of State, Washington, *Told by the Pioneers*. 3 v. Olympia, 1937.

Steamship Historical Society of America, *The Lytle List*, Mystic, Conn., 1952.

Tacoma Harbor When the Wheat is Moving, Tacoma Sunday Ledger Magazine, Dec. 17, 1905.

Tugs of the Puget Sound Tugboat Company and How They Operate, Seattle Post-Intelligencer Sunday Magazine, Oct. 22, 1899.

Wright, E. W., *Lewis and Dryden's Marine History of the Pacific Northwest*, Portland, 1895.

Wuesthoff, Albert T., *In Those Days There Were 16 Men in the Fo'c'sle*, Pacific Motorboat, December, 1950.

Yearbook, Marine Engineers' Beneficial Association, Seattle, 1901.

Yearbook, Puget Sound Piling Busters, Seattle, 1950, 1951.